MEMOIRS *of*
Eleanor E. Hondius
of ELKHORN LODGE

Eleanor James feeding a chipmunk.

MEMOIRS *of*
Eleanor E. Hondius
of ELKHORN LODGE

REVISED EDITION

Edited by Nancy P. Thomas

With a new introduction
by James H. Pickering

ESTES PARK MUSEUM
FRIENDS & FOUNDATION, INC. PRESS
Estes Park, Colorado
2018

© 2018 by the Estes Park Museum Friends & Foundation, Inc.
200 Fourth Street, Estes Park, Colorado 80517
All rights reserved

First Edition 1963
Facsimile Edition 2010
Revised Edition 2018

Printed in the United States of America

The paper used in this publication meets the minimum requirements of the American National Standard for Information Sciences—Permanence of Paper for Printed Library Materials.
ANSI Z39.48-1992

Library of Congress Control Number: 2017935282
ISBN: 978-0-9847780-4-1

Designed and typeset by Pratt Brothers Composition

DEDICATION FOR
THE FIRST EDITION

I am dedicating this book to my son, Pieter,
hoping that he will find things in it
to amuse and entertain him.

Also, I want him to know that he has been a
great comfort to me and a wonderful son.

Eleanor Estes James Hondius
1963

Eleanor James riding her bicycle at Elkhorn Lodge, c. 1900.
IMAGE COURTESY OF ESTES PARK MUSEUM. 2003.006.001

CONTENTS

Preface to the 2010 Facsimile Edition   ix
Introduction to the Revised Edition   xi
Editor's Note   xxiii

ONE Hearsay and History   3
TWO Early Days at Elkhorn Lodge   7
THREE Childhood   12
FOUR Schooldays   23
FIVE Family and Friends   30
SIX Entertainment at Elkhorn   62
SEVEN Elkhorn Guests   85
EIGHT Epilogue   89

Annotated Index   91

Pieter Hondius, Jr., aboard ship, 1943.
IMAGE COURTESY OF ESTES PARK MUSEUM. 1985.063.398

PREFACE TO THE 2010
FACSIMILE EDITION

My mother would be pleased with this republishing of her memoirs. She would also have been pleased with the success of the Estes Park Museum and its contribution to the accurate recounting of the history of the settlement and development of the area through the carefully researched work of historian and Estes Park Laureate Jim Pickering and the Museum staff.

The woman who actually wrote the text and arranged for the original printing of the memoirs, Lorena E. Darby of Longmont, deserves to have a book about herself. She was not only a gifted writer (the text sounds like my mother speaking) but was also a mountaineer and a respected State Senator.

On a personal note, I was not aware that her memoirs were going to become a book. The plan

PREFACE TO THE FACSIMILE EDITION

was to keep my mother occupied since she could no longer be physically active. I was not invited to read the manuscript, and it was a bit of a shock to find myself in print. However, the only correction I would offer is that LSTs [Landing Ship, Tank] did not have sonar.

Pieter Hondius
ESTES PARK
OCTOBER 2009

INTRODUCTION TO
THE REVISED EDITION

Eleanor Hondius' *Memoirs* is a modest sort of book, an unembellished anecdotal narrative written late in life to tell the story of her own family and that of her husband, Dutch-born Pieter Hondius, and the story of the growth and the development of Estes Park. Above all it is the story of Elkhorn Lodge, the oldest surviving resort in the Estes Valley—an historical record that spans some ninety years. "Because I am perhaps the oldest living pioneer in the Estes Park area," she begins, "my son and my friends have asked me to write my memories of Estes Park and Elkhorn Lodge." What follows is a warm, charming, and historically important document.

Born in 1880 in Longmont, where for a number of years the Jameses made their winter home, Eleanor Estes James Hondius quite literally grew

INTRODUCTION TO THE REVISED EDITION

Studio photo of Eleanor Estes James, c. 1883.
IMAGE COURTESY OF ESTES PARK MUSEUM. 1985.063.277

up with Estes Park. Over the course of her lifetime, Mrs. Hondius both watched and participated as a tiny mountain settlement developed into one of the best-known and most popular tourist destinations in Colorado and the West. Except for summers, the

INTRODUCTION TO THE REVISED EDITION

Estes Park of Eleanor's youth was a quiet and sparsely-populated place. Until the mid-1880s, when there were enough year-round residents to justify a community building, which also served as church and school, Estes Park consisted of little more than a series of outlying ranches and small resort hotels, operated by individuals very much like her father, William E. James. In late 1873 or early 1874, James, a man still in his early thirties, had come out to Colorado from Syracuse, New York, and then wandered into the Estes Valley during a hunting trip. Deciding to stay on to ranch and farm, James took up a homestead claim off what is now Devils Gulch Road. (What no doubt attracted him to the spot was its close proximity to the sheltering rocks of Lumpy Ridge, and the fact that a good spring ran close by.) Here he built a small one-room, dirt-roofed log cabin (which still stands), and then brought his wife, Ella McCabe James, and their three small children, all sons under seven, out from Syracuse to their new home.

One winter in a cabin that leaked dirty water when it snowed or rained, Eleanor Hondius explains, was more than enough for her mother. A fortuitous and face-saving swap of properties with the Reverend William McCreery followed, and by April of 1877, William James had relocated his family to land along Fall River, just west of what would become, in the years after 1905, the village of Estes Park. Their new quarters, though larger, were still modest: a frame cabin consisting of a living room, kitchen, and two bedrooms.

As was the case with so many of their neighbors, the Spragues, the MacGregors, and the Fergusons among them, William James soon discovered that although it might be possible to earn a modest living raising cattle, the lodging and feeding of tourist visitors who arrived in increasing numbers each summer offered a more predictable, though scarcely easier, source of livelihood.

And so it began. The Jameses' original homestead cabin gave way to a lodge with parlor and dining room and surrounded by a cluster of cabins and tent houses. By 1880, the fledgling resort was large enough to take care of thirty-five to forty guests. By 1885,

xiii

INTRODUCTION TO THE REVISED EDITION

an enlarged dining room could seat about eighty, and by 1890, a new log building, known as "the Casino," had been added near the eastern entrance to the lodge grounds. The Casino offered additional recreational amenities including its use as a clubhouse for the Elkhorn's nine-hole links golf course, whose first tee box was located nearby. The final improvement, a new and much larger central lodge, came about 1900, to which substantial wings would later be added.

William James, it turned out, played the role of host to perfection, and much of Elkhorn Lodge's early success, as contemporaries pointed out, was due to his "gentlemanly ways and kindly disposition." James, like many early settlers, had a passion for hunting, as the large piles of antlers, the signature feature of Elkhorn Lodge, readily attested. His adventures, which on occasion took him into Wyoming, were put to good use, for after dinner, when guests were gathered around the hearth or bonfire, "Mr. James' hunting stories . . . form[ed] not a little part of the evening's entertainment."

Eleanor Hondius' first chapter, "Hearesay and History," is precisely that, especially when it comes to the (largely apocryphal) stories about the Earl of Dunraven, some of which she admittedly borrowed from Enos Mills' *The Story of Estes Park* (1905). Equally apocryphal is the humorous anecdote about Mr. Chapin ("for whom Mt. Chapin was named"). When Frederick Chapin visited Estes Park during the summers of 1886, 1887, and 1888, his base of operations was Horace Ferguson's Highlands Hotel, located below Marys Lake, not the Elkhorn Lodge. From this point on, however, she is on much surer ground, and much of what she has to say about the world she knew first-hand as a girl, and then as a young adult and woman, is unavailable from other sources. This is particularly true of her colorful anecdotes about such important early-day figures as: the Reverend Elkanah J. Lamb, the Park's first regular minister; postmaster John Cleave, an Englishman from Cornwall; and Johnny Adams, who came to the lodge at eighteen as a stable boy and stayed on to homestead farther west along Fall

xiv

INTRODUCTION TO THE REVISED EDITION

Tent houses and cabins provided additional accommodations for guests at Elkhorn Lodge beginning in the 1880s, c. 1893.
IMAGE COURTESY OF ESTES PARK MUSEUM. 1981.041.001

River. It is also true of what she has to say about her own early years, about her older brothers, Homer and Howard James, who together with her mother assumed responsibility for operating Elkhorn Lodge in the years after William James' death in 1895, and, of course, about her husband, Pieter Hondius, another pioneer, who arrived in Estes Park in 1895 and quickly became one of the area's largest landowners. Pieter and Eleanor were married in 1904.

Particularly valuable is what Eleanor Hondius tells us about Elkhorn Lodge and its development, the guests who stayed there (many of whom loyally returned year after year), how they were fed, housed, and entertained, and, not infrequently, how they entertained themselves. As the reader will discover, there is a great deal of interest in these pages—much of it new to the historical record, all of it delightful.

A valuable postscript to Eleanor's narrative is now available in the large, leather-bound Elkhorn Lodge guest register, donated to

INTRODUCTION TO THE REVISED EDITION

William and Ella James' guests enjoying banjo music on the porch that ran the full length of the original lodge building, c. 1900.
IMAGE COURTESY OF ESTES PARK MUSEUM. 1969.040.014

the Estes Park Museum and now part of its permanent collection. It begins on June 18, 1880, the year of Eleanor's birth and ends in 1914, the year that Europe erupted into what would soon become World War I. Through its pages one can observe the growing popularity of Elkhorn Lodge, particularly after the completion of its new main building in 1900, and the comings and goings of many of those guests who became part of Eleanor's recollections. These include the often-mentioned Sherwood Crocker, the son of Frank and Helen Crocker, who purchased and then renamed the John Stuyvesant ranch below Mount Olympus. It is interesting, perhaps even suggestive, to note that Sherwood, five years Eleanor's senior, is mentioned far more often than his younger sister Helen, who was Eleanor's own age. Also interesting is the wide variety of far-off cities and places from which the Elkhorn drew its guests during the early 1880s—a sign certainly of the growing attractiveness of Estes Park as a destination resort community.

There are any number of historical nuggets as well. We now know with some precision the dates that early photographers like

INTRODUCTION TO THE REVISED EDITION

J. R. Riddle of Topeka, Kansas, and F. E. Baker of Greeley visited Estes Park (almost certainly with the purpose of taking photographs that have long-since become classics). We also know that F. O. Stanley, who entered Estes Park history on the afternoon of June 30, 1903, having successfully maneuvered his small steam car up the rough wagon road from Lyons, spent his very first night in the village at the Elkhorn Lodge.

Beginning in 1890 Eleanor began adding her own name ("Eleanor Estes James") into the ledger in large hand, perhaps as a way of practicing penmanship, but offering a glimpse of the girlhood precocity that would be translated over time into adulthood and, many year later, into the pages of her memoirs.

Not surprisingly, Mrs. Hondius talks with considerable pride about her son, Pieter, named after his father, the individual who graciously authored the Preface to the Friends Press facsimile edition published in 2010. Nearly six decades after writing her memoirs, Eleanor would be even prouder to know that in recent years the National Park Service and other organizations have honored "Pete" Hondius, as he is now affectionately known, for his efforts to protect and preserve the natural beauty of the mountain world that his grandfather and his father entered upon a century and more ago. Pieter Hondius, Jr., was also the recipient of the Estes Park Museum Friends' 2013 Pioneer Award. This too is part of the James-Hondius story.

To be sure, like all autobiographical narratives, Eleanor Hondius is selective in what she chooses to include and also to leave out. There is, in short, much more about Eleanor, her family, and the history of Elkhorn Lodge that we would like to know. For example, we would like to know more about Pieter Hondius' ranching days in Horseshoe Park and in Upper Beaver Meadows, where the Hondius ranch house was located and where Pieter built what was said to be the largest barn in Larimer County to take care of the large herd of cattle he brought up from the valley each spring over the old Bald Mountain-Pole Hill road. Also missing are examples

xvii

INTRODUCTION TO THE REVISED EDITION

Eleanor James, photographed here with a book and a large hat. IMAGE COURTESY OF ESTES PARK MUSEUM.

of the family's generosity, including Eleanor's gift to the Estes Park Library (now the Estes Valley Public Library) in memory of her husband, where to this day a room (the Hondius Room) is named in his honor. Also missing is the story of Pieter Hondius' 1916 gift of $5,000 to the fiscally-strapped Charles Edwin Hewes to keep afloat his foundering Hewes-Kirkwood Inn. This marked the beginning of an intervention that lasted nearly two decades, before Eleanor herself entered into an agreement making it possible for Hewes to rescue the Inn from bankruptcy. The story in all its complexity is one I tell in my 2003 book *In the Vale of Elkanah: The Tahosa Valley*

INTRODUCTION TO THE REVISED EDITION

World of Charles Edwin Hewes. But these are merely the wishes of someone who, having been invited to learn new details of history, is never quite satisfied and always wants to know more.

Much of the *Memoirs'* artistry comes from the unassuming, natural voice that speaks to the reader—one that immediately establishes that sense of authenticity that only first-hand narrative can provide. Yet this voice is not, as Pieter Hondius, Jr., tells us, that of his mother, but rather of her younger friend Lorena E. Darby (1914–1993) of Longmont. Mrs. Darby, it turns out, was an enormously talented woman in her own right. Not only did she represent Boulder County in the forty-ninth and fiftieth sessions of the Colorado Senate, from 1973 to 1976, but also, as publisher and part owner of the *Longmont Ledger* between 1964 and 1969, she authored a series of columns collected and published in 1972 as *Mountains and Molehills.* The title of her small book is instructive. It suggests that ghost-writer Lorena Darby, if that in fact is what she was, was not unlike Eleanor Hondius herself: someone who, however much involved in the tasks of living, kept things very much in perspective. This is most certainly true of her achievement here, for as Pieter Hondius adds, "the text sounds like my mother speaking."

Eleanor James Hondius died in 1968, five years after the publication of a book that for many years was out of print, difficult to find, and expensive to purchase until the Friends Press republished a facsimile in 2010. Eight years later, this revised edition has allowed me to consider Eleanor's *Memoirs* with fresh eyes and revise this introduction. What has not changed, of course, is the narrative itself. Those interested in the history of Estes Park, the history of the James and Hondius families, and the history of Elkhorn Lodge are once again very much indebted to Pieter Hondius, Jr., for allowing the Press of the Estes Park Museum Friends & Foundation, Inc., to republish his mother's wonderful *Memoirs.* We are also indebted to the Press' Editor-in-Chief, Nancy P. Thomas, who facilitated the

INTRODUCTION TO THE REVISED EDITION

production of the 2010 and 2018 editions and the enhancement of the work through the addition of an index as well as many new photographs from the collections of the Estes Park Museum. Many of these are gifts to the Museum from Pieter, Jr., and his family.

James H. Pickering
HISTORIAN LAUREATE, TOWN OF ESTES PARK
2018

Eleanor Estes James, wedding photo. She and Pieter Hondius were married on Nov. 9, 1904, in Los Angeles, California.
IMAGE COURTESY OF ESTES PARK MUSEUM. 1985.063.276

EDITOR'S NOTE

This book is a revised edition of the *Memoirs of Eleanor E. Hondius of Elkhorn Lodge,* published first in 1963 and reprinted as a facsimile copy by the Estes Park Museum Friends & Foundation, Inc., Press in 2010. Although every effort has been made to retain the character and tone of the original work and to preserve Eleanor's original text, some changes to punctuation have been made to improve clarity and readability. Almost all of the photographs Eleanor chose for her book will also be found in this revised version; however, some been rescanned from originals found in the Estes Park Museum, and others may have been rearranged or resized. (For example, photographs that appeared in a "Publishers' note" following the Epilogue in Eleanor's 1963 edition now appear where appropriate within the text.) In addition,

EDITOR'S NOTE

new photographs, many from the Hondius family and now held by the Museum, have been added. Editorial additions or corrections other than punctuation changes appear in brackets.

Finally, the revised edition contains an index, which provides full names, dates, and notes that clarify people, places, and events mentioned in the text. While these would have been easily recognized by readers of Eleanor's original book, they may not be familiar to today's readers.

Nancy Pickering Thomas
EDITOR-IN CHIEF, MUSEUM FRIENDS PRESS
2018

FACING PAGE. *Eleanor playfully balances her puppy on a book, in front of the Lodge porch, c. 1900.* IMAGE COURTESY OF ESTES PARK MUSEUM. 1985.063.164

MEMOIRS of
Eleanor E. Hondius
of ELKHORN LODGE

The Estes valley as it looked from Pole Hill, before the Big Thompson River was dammed to create Lake Estes.

CHAPTER ONE

Hearsay and History

Because I am perhaps the oldest living pioneer of the Estes Park area, my son and my friends have asked me to write my memories of Estes Park and the Elkhorn Lodge.

According to Enos Mills's book, "The Story of Estes Park," the Earl of Dunraven, with his guests Sir William Cunnings [sic] and Earl Fitzpatrick [sic] hunted in Estes Park in the autumn and early winter of 1872.

"Dunraven was so delighted with the abundance of game and the beauty and grandeur of the scenes, that he determined to have Estes Park as a game preserve," writes Mr. Mills.

Lord Dunraven was supposed to have acquired 14,000 acres of land in the Park, most of it by fraudulent means. My mother said that his agents would go out in the streets in Denver, and any

The English Hotel, built by Windham Thomas Wyndham-Quinn, Fourth Earl of Dunraven, in 1877.

man who was willing to sell his homestead rights would receive from $50 to $100 for his right to file on a claim.

Albert Bierstadt, the artist, selected the sites for the Dunraven Hotel and the Dunraven Cottage in 1874, but the buildings were not erected until later. The hotel, destroyed by fire in 1912 [*sic*], went under several names: first, the Dunraven Hotel; later, the English Hotel; and finally, the Estes Park Hotel. The "cottage" built by Dunraven for a home is now the property of the Campfire Girls, and is used as a summer camp. When Mr. Stanley and Mr. Sanborn bought the Dunraven property, they acquired only about 8,000 acres.

The following information I got from Abner Sprague:

The last time Lord Dunraven came to the Park, he brought with him a party of eight, and they all stayed at the Dunraven Hotel. At the hotel that summer was also Joe Jefferson, the actor, and his family.

HEARSAY AND HISTORY

Guests at the English Hotel mount up for a trail ride, c. 1895.
IMAGE COURTESY OF ESTES PARK MUSEUM. R2006.013.502

Among Lord Dunraven's guests was a Lady Florence, who had a little dog. Lady Florence would take her dog to the dining room with her, and put him in a high chair. She would take a bite of food, then feed her dog a bite. The American guests resented this very much, and Joe Jefferson told the manager that unless Lord Dunraven and his party left the hotel, all the American guests would leave. He added that Lady Florence was an actress, and was considered to be one of the worst characters on the boards in England.

Lord Dunraven was quite angry, and said, "I wish I had my papers here; I could show them how I stand with the crowned heads of Europe."

However, he and his guests went to Horseshoe Park on a camping trip, and lived in tents for a month before they left the park. As far as I know, Lord Dunraven never came back to Estes after that, but almost every year some of his English friends would appear.

The Griff Evans family was installed in a cabin known as the Ranchhouse, owned by Lord Dunraven, and were in his employ.

HEARSAY AND HISTORY

They cared for Lord Dunraven and his guests when they came on their hunting trips. Poor Mrs. Evans was driven almost crazy with worry when a number of English friends of Lord Dunraven descended upon her during their hunting expeditions.

In her book, "A Lady's Life in the Rocky Mountains," Isabella Bird writes a great deal about Rocky Mountain Jim. He lived in a cabin near the present Meadowdale Stock Ranch, at the head of Muggins Gulch.

One year, a friend of Lord Dunraven's known as Lord H. came to the Park. According to Mr. Sprague, Mountain Jim acted as guide for Lord H. on a hunting trip. Mountain Jim was considered a very decent fellow as long as he was sober, but was ugly when drunk. The two men evidently had a quarrel, and Lord H. was afraid Jim might kill him.

According to Mr. Sprague, Griff Evans was hired to shoot Mountain Jim, and inflicted a wound that resulted in Jim's death several months later. Griff Evans's trial was held in Ft. Collins; the witnesses were supposed to have been bought off because Evans went free. Mountain Jim died shortly after the trial ended, and the Evans family eventually left the Park.

As a little girl, I remember seeing Mr. and Mrs. John R. Stuyvesant drive by in their buckboard with a span of blooded, frisky horses and six or eight hounds trailing behind them. Mr. Stuyvesant was a direct descendent of "Peg-leg" Peter Stuyvesant, the first governor of New Amsterdam. He bought the claim of Isaak [*sic*] Rowe in 1888, and built the yellow house that still stands at the foot of Mt. Olympus. Mrs. Stuyvesant was a plump little woman; Mr. Stuyvesant was a larger edition.

They were in the Park four or five years, and then the property was deeded to his wife, Elizabeth Ten Eyck Stuyvesant. This property was held by the Stuyvesant estate for many years, and was finally bought by Mr. F. W. Crocker of Denver. On Mr. Crocker's death, he left the estate to his two grandsons, Arthur and Walter Pew of the Sun Oil Co.

CHAPTER TWO

Early Days at Elkhorn Lodge

In late 1873 or early 1874, my father, William E. James, came to Denver and went with some friends on a hunting trip to Estes Park. In those days, there were no roads, no bridges, just a horse trail into the Park. The Indians had already come and gone, and also the Joel Estes family. My father said the elk and deer and mountain sheep "almost ran over you," and he never took a creel when he went fishing. As a little girl, I can remember the men coming in and emptying the fish into a wash tub after two hours' fishing.

My father was so charmed with the Estes Park area that he wrote my mother in Syracuse, N.Y. that he had found a place where he would file on land and make his home. So Mother, with her three little boys: Homer, about six or seven; Charlie, about four; and Howard, the baby, came to Colorado.

William E. and Ella McCabe James, founders of Elkhorn Lodge and parents of Homer, Charles, Howard, and Eleanor Estes James.

There were no direct trains into Denver; Mother and the boys went to Cheyenne, Wyo., and from there on a spur line to Denver.

My father was not at the depot to meet them, so they took a cab to his boarding house, where they found Father in bed with inflamatory rheumatism. His leg was so badly inflamed the doctor wanted to amputate it. But Father said, "I was born with two legs, and I'll die with two legs!"

In about two months, Father was able to be about again. By this time, the family's furniture had arrived from the East, so Father hired someone to take the family and the furniture to Estes Park. It took three days to make the trip from Denver.

The only place they could find to live when they arrived in the Park was a one-room log cabin with a dirt roof on the McCreery ranch. Whenever it snowed, my Father had to clear the snow off the roof, or, as it melted, muddy water would leak through onto the furniture and the family. The log cabin is still standing.

It was very difficult to determine legally what land was available, since most of it was claimed by Lord Dunraven. Father took up a

William and Ella James' sons, from left, Charles, Howard, and Homer, c. 1872.

claim at the upper end of Black Canyon and built a cabin for his family there.

At that time, Mrs. McGregor [sic] was serving as the first postmistress of Estes Park, and the post office was located on the McGregor Ranch. (It was later moved to the building known as the Ranchhouse, occupied by the Griff Evans family.)

Because of some legal technicality, Mrs. McGregor's mother, Mrs. Heeney, "jumped" Father's claim to the land. Although she had no cabin, and her only shelter was a crude log structure, she could hold the claim by sleeping there one night a month.

My mother called Mr. McGregor a "pettifogging" lawyer. I never knew what a "pettifogging" lawyer was, except that Mother

EARLY DAYS AT ELKHORN LODGE

said Mr. McGregor was one. When the final decision on the property came back from Washington, it was in favor of Mrs. Heeney.

At that time in the Park there were several saw mills and a number of lumbermen. These men liked my father and disliked Mr. McGregor. They wanted to tar and feather McGregor and ride him out of town on a rail. But Father said, "No, I've come from a civilized community, and I intend to remain civilized."

That first winter was a very difficult one for our family. Father and a Mr. Rowe supported their families by killing deer and elk and catching fish, which they took to Denver to sell.

The spring of 1875 my Mother's father died and left her some money. By that time, too, new settlers were arriving and squatting on Dunraven land. Father took up land where the Elkhorn Lodge now stands. I've always been grateful to Mrs. Heeney for jumping Father's first claim; otherwise, I'd still be picking chokecherries at the upper end of Black Canyon.

The house they built on the new property consisted of a frame building with two small bedrooms, a living room, dining room, and kitchen.

The family had a big black cat called Tommy. When the time came to move from Black Canyon to the new home, Tommy could not be found. But after the kitchen stove was set up, and a fire started in it, Tommy made his whereabouts known. He was in the oven!

Father had no intention of having a guest ranch; he planned to go into the cattle business. But every summer people came to the ranch and begged to be allowed to stay, and each winter another cabin would be built on the ranch to house them. Father and Mother soon found there was more money in caring for summer tourists than in raising cattle.

⌐

Mother told the story about Mr. Chapin, for whom Mt. Chapin was named. He was a guest one summer, and occupied one of the little bedrooms. He always kept his window open, and every day a hen would come in through the window and lay an egg on his bed.

In those days, eggs were hauled in each week by wagon from the valley; when they arrived, half were broken, and the other half should have been. So Mother kept a few hens at the ranch.

She didn't want Mr. Chapin to know about the hen laying an egg on his bed each day, so she would listen carefully for the hen's cackle, then hastily remove from Mr. Chapin's bed the egg and any feathers the hen might have lost. Each morning Mr. Chapin had a fresh egg for breakfast without ever suspecting where the egg had been laid.

Among the very early visitors at Elkhorn Ranch were Mrs. F. W. Crocker and her infant son of Denver, and Miss Hyde, who was a sister of the Mr. Hyde of Mentholatum fame. The doctor had told Mrs. Crocker to take her baby son, Sherwood, to the mountains where it was cool in order to save his life.

They arrived at our ranchhouse, where Mother refused to take them in because she already had a great deal to do. But when Father heard the story about Sherwood, he said, "Give me that baby. He shall stay here." After a few weeks, Father had Sherwood sitting on his lap eating griddle cakes. From that time, the Crocker family were our very close friends. Miss Hyde started a school at the ranch for my brothers.

CHAPTER THREE

Childhood

I think now I will come into the story. I was born January 6, 1880, in Longmont, Colorado. Mother, having had three boys, was delighted when she was told she had a daughter.

Even as a baby I found myself trying to do things to entertain and amuse the guests. One of the families staying at the ranch the summer after I was born asked my brother to tell Mother, "When the baby wakes up, bring her over to us." From that time on, they cared for me most of the summer.

Six years later, this family returned, and they asked at once to see "the baby," mentioning that they had a box of candy for the baby. I had been told the story of their attachment for me, so I knew I was "the baby." When I heard of their arrival and about the candy, it didn't take me long to make myself known.

CHILDHOOD

Eleanor Estes James, c. 1881.
IMAGE COURTESY OF ESTES
PARK MUSEUM. 1985.063.279.

Tommy, the James family cat.

It must have been a terrible shock to them when they saw me! I had bangs across my forehead; the rest of my head was shingled like a boy's. Mother had no time to fuss with curls; nor did she have time to change my dress or wash my face before I made myself known.

Well, I got the candy, but never again did I hear anyone ask for "the baby."

At the age of six, my only playmate was Tommy, the cat. He was five years older than I and was willing to take life easy. So I could play with him, comb his fur, and take him riding in my doll buggy. The minute the doll clothes came off the doll, they went on Tommy; there he would lie, while I rolled him back and forth.

Still, he must have kept one eye open, because let a chipmunk cross his line of vision, and with one bound, Tommy was after him. The chase usually ended under the house, and when, after much coaxing, Tommy would reappear minus his bonnet and with a badly mutilated dress, I would gather him into my arms and

CHILDHOOD

Eleanor Estes James, c. 1890.
IMAGE COURTESY OF ESTES PARK MUSEUM. 1985.063.281

change his clothes, and clean his fur. I even taught him to sit in a high chair, with a napkin around his neck, to eat his meals.

Every once in a while, the stage would bring a lone tourist to Estes Park, and there would be no place for him to stay, so we would take him in. One time I remember a young man came. My brother Charlie, who died when he was twenty years old, went out and caught trout for the evening meal. Mother saw to it that a tempting supper was served, and everyone was on his best behavior.

I begged Mother to let me take Tommy to the table in his high chair. She said in a shocked voice, "I should say not!" But I begged so hard, with tears in my eyes, that she finally relented.

The seating arrangement was something like this: the guest, then Tommy in his high chair, then me. Tommy, with his napkin around his neck, behaved beautifully. I had boned his trout for him, and he ate daintily. Then I saw him casting glances at his neighbor's plate. Before I could stop him, Tommy had reached out a paw, caught the guest's trout by the tail, and pulled it over to his plate, where he went to work on it.

I was so delighted with the cute thing Tommy had done that I burst out laughing. This was the wrong thing, because it called the attention of all the rest to what Tommy had done. Well, both Tommy and I were sent from the table.

Although after a fashion I could read, my reading was very limited. One of our visitors felt sorry for me and sent me Lewis Carroll's "Alice in Wonderland" and "Through the Looking Glass." No one ever enjoyed these books more than I did. They had to be read to me, but I learned them practically by heart.

"'Will you walk a little faster?' said the whiting to the snail. 'There's a porpoise close behind us, and he's treading on my tail!'"

Our winter life in Estes Park was a quiet, simple one. There were few people living in the area, and we had to make our own amusement. My father, who thought that only New York State could grow proper apples, would have a couple barrels of apples sent from the East—Northern Spy or Russets. There would also be small bags of hazelnuts and butternuts, and there was always a five-gallon jug of sweet cider on the premises.

In the long evenings, we would gather in the living room where my Father would sit in his comfortable chair and smoke his cigar.

CHILDHOOD

J.R. Riddle's photo of Jameses' parlors at Elkhorn lodge, c. 1884. The room at the south end featured a bay window and a rosewood piano.
IMAGE COURTESY OF THE ESTES PARK MUSEUM. 1985.063.245.

The first boy to get to the couch could keep it. We always had a roaring fire in the fireplace, because this was the only means of heating the room. The wind would be howling outside, joined by an occasional chorus of coyotes; on the hearth we would put apples to roast before the fire and the boys would crack nuts. Sometimes they would pop corn, and there was always sweet cider to drink. Then Mother would read to us by the light of a coal-oil lamp; it was usually a novel full of romance, which was the type of book she preferred.

At nine or half-past, we all had to pick up our lamps and go to bed, because we had to be up by six o'clock the next morning. Occasionally, some of the other settlers would come to the Lodge to have a meal with us; now and then some stayed overnight.

When summer came, I had the guests' children to play with, and because I was a tomboy and could climb and ride horseback, I

Women playing tennis at Elhorn Lodge, 1895. Oldman Mountain can be seen in the background.
IMAGE COURTESY OF ESTES PARK MUSEUM. 1984.036.002

was popular with the children—though not too popular with their parents.

One of the first troubles I got them into was when I introduced them to my brothers' swimming pool in the river nearby. This was long before the days of bikinis; we simply undressed in the bushes and went swimming in our birthday suits.

Not having any snow to throw at each other, we threw sand. We had a hilarious time, and made so much noise that parents and maids looking for the children soon found us. Some of us were spanked, some were shaken, some were scolded; but all were made to go into the bushes and put on our clothes. From that time, the swimming pool was "off bounds" for all of us. Of course, I was blamed for the whole affair.

Most of the children rode ponies. I had a little roly-poly pony called Bessie, and I rode bareback. Whenever Bessie stopped or stumbled, I rolled off; but I never got hurt, because I was so close to the ground anyway.

At night, most of the children went to bed at 8 or 8:30. I objected to such an early bedtime, so I would hide from my mother, and thereby see a great many things I was not supposed to see. The next day, members of the grapevine would seek me out and say, "Little girl, where were you last night when your mother was looking for you, and what did you see?"

Knowing what was expected of me, if I had no information to pass on, I manufactured some. My reward was having the questioners look at each other and say, "What an awful child!"

There was always mountain climbing to be done. We practically lived on Old Man Mountain just behind the Lodge. In the middle of his "stomach" was a crack that went across the entire mountain. At the center, the crack was so wide we could drop down into sort of a cave. This was a grand place to explore, to build a fire, roast potatoes and fry meat. Every few days we went to the cave on Old Man Mountain for our lunch.

When I was about eleven or twelve years old, a family from Chicago came to stay at the Lodge. They had a very nice boy about my age, and by this time I had found a better place to cook our lunch at the cave.

One day I was busy frying the potatoes while my companion went down to the river to get water. Suddenly, the grease in the frying pan caught fire, and the pan was in flames. I went to the door of the cave and hurled the whole thing out just as the boy came in. Hot grease splattered his hands and face. The boy began to cry.

I wasn't accustomed to a crying boy, so I washed my hands of the whole affair and started for home. The boy followed me and begged me to turn around and go back. But I was adamant; I went home.

A rainy day many years later while sitting before the fireplace at the Elkhorn talking with my guests, the clerk came to tell me there was a man at the desk who wanted to see me. When I got to the office, there stood a fine-looking man, much younger than I, smiling at me.

CHILDHOOD

He said, "Don't you know me?"

"No," I replied, "should I?"

"Yes; we kept house together!"

It was the boy into whose face I had thrown the potatoes. I invited him in and we had a fine time talking about that summer. He was staying with a family from Chicago who had a summer home near Longs Peak Inn. I never saw him again.

⸺

The summer I was sixteen, I spent almost the entire summer with the Borden family from Chicago. They were not the Bordens of condensed milk fame; Mr. Borden was a lawyer.

The eldest son, John, was about my age; Mary was about fifteen, and William was about twelve. Mrs. Borden was a very religious woman; she had a Sunday school every Sunday in her cottage, and I was invited to attend. The rest of the week, we rode horseback practically the entire time. In the evening, I taught John to dance.

They never returned to Elkhorn, but I kept in touch with the family. John Borden was the father of Ellen Borden, former wife of Adlai Stevenson. Mary Borden went to England, married two different Englishmen, and wrote novels. William Borden, who graduated from Harvard, was the only religious one of the family. After leaving college, he went as a missionary to India, and later contracted a fever and died in Egypt. Someone wrote the story of his life, called "Borden of Harvard." A copy of the book was sent to me.

⸺

As a young woman at the Lodge, I was kept busy in the summer riding horseback. Sometimes all the good horses would be taken, and sometimes there were no horses at all left in the stable. Then I would have to stay home.

I complained bitterly to my mother about this situation, and finally she bought me a horse, Patsy, from Mr. Cole who had a ranch on beyond Longs Peak Inn. The horse was well-bred, but

CHILDHOOD

Eleanor James astride patsy, her favorite horse, n.d.
IMAGE COURTESY OF ESTES PARK MUSEUM. 2006.006.004_45

had never been properly broken to the side-saddle; in those days a modest girl never rode astride.

So Mr. Cole put on a skirt and trained my horse. One day he brought Patsy to the Lodge, saying he thought she was ready for me to ride. Mother insisted that the stableboy ride Patsy first; she immediately bucked him off.

I made friends with Patsy by feeding her candy, patting her and talking to her, and one day the side-saddle was put on. Although she did not like the skirt and always kept one eye on it, from that time on, we had no trouble. The only bad habit Patsy had was that she would shy at a wet spot in the road or when a chipmunk jumped out from the bank. I always found I was more secure then in the side-saddle than when I rode with the Western saddle.

There were times when I would offer Patsy to some young man to exercise. She would take him a couple of miles from Elkhorn,

CHILDHOOD

Eleanor preferred to ride Patsy using a side-saddle because she felt more secure than she did in a western saddle.
IMAGE COURTESY OF ESTES PARK MUSEUM. 2003.006.005-14

then buck him off. She would come home with the reins dangling, wearing a pleased expression, as much as to say, "I got rid of him!" It was not long until I was the only one who rode Patsy.

When I went into the office and had no time for riding, little Patsy went into the general livery with about 110 other horses. One summer she came home from pasture with a colt; she lost her slender graceful lines and became quite matronly. Gradually, she was just one of the horses in the livery.

༄

As a young lady, my evening duties at the Lodge included dancing with the wallflowers at the Casino, and from time to time, having a little attention shown me. At that time, I weighed about 115 pounds, and although not beautiful, I was full of life and had a good time.

Many years later, after my husband died and I weighed about 188 pounds, the room clerk came to my cottage one day and said, "Mrs. Hondius, an old beau of yours is here to see you."

CHILDHOOD

Eleanor James, c. 1903.
IMAGE COURTESY OF ESTES PARK MUSEUM. 1985.063.331

"Tell him I'm not here," I answered. "Then he can keep his illusions."

"Oh, no, this is just a former guest who has asked to see you or Mr. James," protested the clerk.

I went over; there stood a man on the porch, grinning away. When I came to the steps, these were his words: "And so this is *little* Ella."

I could have killed that room clerk!

CHAPTER FOUR

Schooldays

The first school to be opened in Estes Park was held in one of the three-room cottages at the Elkhorn. There were very few children in Estes Park at that time, and I believe I was the only girl. I was about three years old. My father hired a man to teach the boys, and the teacher got his board and lodging at Elkhorn.

After about two or three years, Father decided there were enough people in the park so that a district school could be established, and obtained permission for the building of a district school.

The school was built on the site where the Estes Park bank is now located. Part of the old building has been moved west on Main Street and is used by Mrs. Frumess and her son as a gift shop. The work of constructing the school was done by Mr. Cleve [sic], my Father, and my older brother.

SCHOOLDAYS

Eleanor James attended the first Estes Park school.
IMAGE COURTESY OF ESTES PARK MUSEUM. 1985.063.275.

Of course the school building was used for all public gatherings, as well as for school. At election time, it was used as a polling place. On the day of election, at seven o'clock, Mr. Cleve would appear at the door of the school with a school bell; he would ring the bell lustily and say, "Hear ye, hear ye; the polling place of the United States is now open. Come ye and vote." Then he would ring the bell again and disappear.

At that time, I doubt if there were more than seventy or eighty voters in the Park; some came from Devil's [sic] Gulch and some

SCHOOLDAYS

from Muggins Gulch. They were nearly all Republicans; in fact, I only know of one family of Democrats who lived in the Park at that time. Then there were two men, Enos Mills and John Adams, who were called "Mugwumps." I never really knew what a Mugwump was; it is possible they were not affiliated with any party, but cast their vote as they pleased.

From time to time, we would have a social gathering in the school house, and occasionally, a visiting minister would preach a sermon there.

Finally, the Rev. Elkanah Lamb became our regular minister; in fact, he appointed himself saying, "As long as there are eight or ten people gathered together in the name of the Lord, I will preach."

He was of the United Brethren sect, and certainly a great believer in hellfire and damnation; his sermons were never less than an hour in length.

He was at least six feet five inches tall, and he wore a long black frock on Sunday. On the table, which served as a pulpit, he would lay a snowy white handkerchief. As he preached, his voice would get louder and louder, and finally he was shouting. Suddenly, he would stop, pick up the handkerchief, and give his nose a violent blow. (I always thought this trumpeting would put Gabriel to shame.) Then Mr. Lamb would start the sermon again, and go back up the scale.

We had another United Brethren minister who lived in the community and attended the services. One day he objected to some remark about [St.] Paul. Mrs. Lamb, who was sitting near the stove, suffering with rheumatism, and had had all the sermon she could stand, said: "What did Paul know about women, anyway? He was never married."

That ended the sermon for that day.

I played the organ for the church services, and such an organ! The front panels would shake and quiver as I pumped my feet like

SCHOOLDAYS

The Rev. Elkanah Lamb (1831– 1915), c. 1890. IMAGE COURTESY OF ESTES PARK MUSEUM. 1966.011.005

Jemima Jane Spencer Lamb (1829– 1917), c. 1890. IMAGE COURTESY OF ESTES PARK MUSEUM. 1966.011.006

mad to get air into the bellows. If ever there was an antique, it was that organ.

One fall, I said to my Mother, "Can't you give me a job? I'd like to have some money of my own." The only job she would trust me with was washing the breakfast dishes.

One Sunday morning, I had a lot of dishes to wash, and about three-quarters of a mile to walk to get to church. When I arrived, the services had started and the congregation was praying.

I opened the door and crept in, hoping that I had not been noticed, only to hear the Rev. Lamb say, "Dear Lord, forgive these lazy, good-for-nothing people who can not get up early enough on Sunday morning to get to church on time." I was furious and decided *he* could play the old organ.

When the prayer was over, he looked up and said, mildly "Now, Elly, we'll sing hymn number one. . . ." I went to the organ and played the accompaniment for "Holy, Holy, Holy."

SCHOOLDAYS

Studio photo of "Elly" James c. 1885.
IMAGE COURTESY OF ESTES PARK MUSEUM. 1985.063.314A

Mr. Cleve always took up the collection. One Sunday during the late summer, a Mr. Garner, a wealthy man from the East, put $50 in the collection plate. After the service was over, Mr. Cleve went to him and asked him if he hadn't made a mistake and offered to return the $50.

When the World's Fair [1889] was held in Paris, the Rev. Lamb and Enos Mills went to Europe to attend the fair. It seems that when it came time to cross the English Channel, the two men got separated. Enos Mills got on the English boat, but the Rev. Lamb got on a French vessel, and could not understand the people on the boat. But he showed his passport, and they took him across the Channel.

SCHOOLDAYS

The two vessels arrived in port about the same time, so the Rev. Lamb and Enos Mills got together again.

They had a great deal of difficulty seeing the Fair because they could not speak French. They found it hard to make themselves understood, especially when it came to eating. They tried and tried to order beefsteak, but when the order was placed before them, it was always chicken in some form or other.

From Paris they went to Italy, and decided to climb Mt. Vesuvius. The authorities insisted they must have a guide, which seemed very unnecessary to them. Hadn't they played leapfrog on Longs Peak most of their lives? As they argued, some soldiers came up with fixed bayonets, so the two men decided to take along a guide.

When they returned to France, Enos Mills wanted to see some more of the Continent, but Mr. Lamb said he wanted to get back to "God-speaking people," so he went to England to wait for Enos. He later said, "While Enos was on the Continent and I was with God-speaking people—that was the pleasantest part of the whole trip."

When he returned to Estes Park, he gave a lecture on his journey, and I was always sorry that it could not have been taken down in his own words.

The Rev. Lamb finally wrote a book on his life, with the title "Memories of the Future and Thoughts of the Past." After it was printed, someone called his attention to the title, so he had another edition printed with "past" and "future" exchanging places.

In this book, he referred to a girl he loved dearly in his youth. He said he had loved her all of his life, had never been able to forget her, and doubted that he would through all eternity. A few pages later, he wrote, "I married the present Mrs. E. J. Lamb in September, 1868." I couldn't forgive him for this, for if ever there was a faithful, devoted wife, Mrs. Lamb was that person.

For two or three winters there met in the schoolhouse a group known as the Literary Society of Estes Park. Johnny Adams was

SCHOOLDAYS

the president, and I was secretary-treasurer. Anybody who wanted to be a member was welcome; the only requirement was that members contribute to the entertainment. For instance, Mrs. Talent [*sic*], the mother of Lee Talent [*sic*], wrote poetry fluently; Mrs. Abner Sprague and her sister-in-law, Mrs. Chapman, sang duets.

However, the main contributor was Warren Rutledge, who had just come into possession of one of those wonderful phonographs which had to be wound and had a huge horn. Just let there be a pause in the program, and Warren Rutledge would leap to the rescue, and we'd have "In the Shade of the Old Apple Tree," or "Silver Threads Among the Gold," or the song about Casey, who danced with the strawberry blond. Sometimes it seemed to us that it was more of a concert than a literary society.

After the literary part was over, we had a basket social, which was really what most of the people came for. All the women would fill baskets or boxes with the most tempting food they could think of, and then the baskets and boxes would be put up for auction and go to the highest bidder. Sometimes if you wanted a certain person to know which was your box, you decorated it with a geranium blossom, and wore another as a boutonniere.

After three years, this literary society was discontinued, and we bought a second-hand upright piano for the school with the money we had raised from the box socials.

CHAPTER FIVE

Family and Friends

The Cleves

After the Evans family left the Park, Mr. Cleve, who was employed by Lord Dunraven as a carpenter and who had helped to build the old English or Dunraven Hotel, lived at the Ranchhouse. He married an aunt of Mrs. Shep Husted, and they had one child, Paul.

About two years later, Mrs. Cleve was going to have another child. This upset Mr. Cleve who wanted no more children, and he raised such a hubub that Mrs. Cleve agreed there would be no more. After that, Mr. Cleve took his meals with the family, but lived in the two-room building across the road which was used as a post office and store. Eventually, however, his daughter, Virginia, became his favorite child.

FAMILY AND FRIENDS

Johnny Adams (left) with his brother George, at George's cabin, which was located on Fall River, a few yards east of what is now Nicky's Resort. IMAGE COURTESY OF ESTES PARK MUSEUM. 1980.036.001

Mr. Cleve kept the store as an accommodation for the summer people. However, he had favorites he protected. For instance, he always kept for Mother a five-pound box of chocolate creams which she served on the dessert menu at the Lodge. Then there was George Adams, who had to be supplied with chewing tobacco. When he found this delicacy was becoming exhausted, Mr. Cleve would say to the other customers, "George will be coming for some soon." Sherwood Crocker and my brother, Howard, would buy ten cents worth of candy, and when that was gone they would try to get more, Mr. Cleve would exclaim, "Dash it, fellows, you dinna want to chew it—you want to suck it!"

The truth of the matter was that he found it a great nuisance having to replenish the stock of the store.

FAMILY AND FRIENDS

Eventually Mr. Cleve was given land by Lord Dunraven where the town of Estes Park now stands. The family had its dwelling where the hotel is, and his post office and store was located on the corner now occupied by the Chez Jay building.

Many funny stories were told of people coming to the post office for their mail, and running into an argument between Mr. and Mrs. Cleve. She would send the children over to their father at the store to get some butter, and he would say, "What is the bugger doing with all that butter? Tell your mother she can't have any."

When the children got part way home, he would decide that the best diplomacy was to give them something, so he would call them back and give them a pound of soda. The exchange went back and forth, because Mrs. Cleve knew what she wanted, and usually got it eventually.

⌐

At one time, I ran into some difficulty with the Cleve family. We had some neighbors, the Johnson brothers, who were living on the McGregor ranch and had a lot of chickens. One cold winter night, a coyote got into the chicken house and killed about twenty hens before Eddie Johnson could get his gun and dispose of the coyote. He said the coyote would grab one chicken by the neck and kill it, then another and another. It was a very cold night, and by morning the dead chickens were frozen. It wasn't long before the neighbors heard of the raid on the Johnson chickenhouse.

The Johnsons didn't know what to do with the dead chickens. I suggested that they pick them and clean them and bring them to me at the Elkhorn and I would make pressed chicken of them.

Mother had a large new clothes boiler, and into this I put the chickens. It took me the better part of two days to cook them and to separate the meat from the bones. Then I chopped the meat and packed it into four milk pans. The broth was seasoned with sage and salt and pepper and cooked until slightly jelled, and then poured over the chicken. The Johnson boys refused to take more than two milk pans of the pressed chicken, so I decided to give some to the Cleves.

I found you could overdo a good thing; by being too generous, I made my mistake. I sent the Cleves half a milk pan of pressed chicken. It didn't take them long to decide where the chicken came from, and you would have thought I was trying to poison them. When I tried to tell Mrs. Cleve how sanitarily the chicken had been prepared, she exclaimed, "But just think what violent deaths they died!"

However, the Cleves finally forgave me. They were very good neighbors, and of course Mr. Cleve was a good Republican. The two large lilac bushes outside the front of the dining room at the Elkhorn Lodge he brought to us. He dug the holes and planted them, but not until he had brought some proper dirt from his meadows; he did not consider the dirt at the Lodge good enough for them.

Oyster Supper

The people in the Park who stayed all winter sometimes found it very long, so they had an oyster supper or some other entertainment now and then to break the monotony. Because Elkhorn Lodge was centrally located, they usually held these get-togethers at Elkhorn.

This party I'm going to tell you about was an oyster supper. Pails of oysters had been ordered and kept on ice. Two captains had been chosen; those men who were willing and able to hunt had been chosen to alternately be the captains. The team of hunters which brought in the least game would pay for the oysters.

The points for the game had been listed pretty much like this: elk topped the list, although none had been seen for years in the Park; next came bear, which of course were now in hibernation; the value of the points went down to the lowly chipmunk.

About seven or eight o'clock in the morning, the hunters started out. The women and children and the men who did not hunt came to the Elkhorn about two o'clock in the afternoon to make preparations for the evening. Tables were set, and a huge fire was built in the fireplace in the dining room to heat the big room.

About five o'clock in the evening, I went to get some wood for the fireplace. I saw a man with a gun coming down the hill behind the cottages, walking stealthily and all doubled up. It was my brother, Homer, who had started out to kill an elk in the morning, and was now trying to bag a squirrel. I think jackrabbits were about the largest game brought in.

At 5:30, all of the hunters had returned except Fred Sprague, a member of my brother Homer's team. He was never known to hunt and was a notorious yarner, so his teammates did not have much hope. At six o'clock he appeared, and assured the men he had killed a deer. Where was it?

He had wounded it and had followed it for miles, he reported. The deer, he said, had bled profusely, so he had been able to follow it, up one hill and down another, around that rock pile, and through that clump of trees. It had finally grown too dark to follow the trail any further. "Tomorrow I'll go out and bring in that deer!" he promised.

But everyone was satisfied that my brother's team should pay for the oysters. After the oysters had been eaten—raw, stewed, and scalloped—and the women had cleared the dining room, some of the guests played cards, others danced.

Among the group was the Rev. Baldwin, a United Brethren minister. He decided the evening was taking on a wicked hue, and said to his wife, "Now we must go home so I can milk the cow."

Mrs. Baldwin, who was having the time of her life and did not have many times like this, replied, "No. You can milk that cow just as well tomorrow morning as you can at ten o'clock tonight."

The party did not break up until one or two o'clock in the morning. In those days we had much more snow in the Park than we have now, and it was very cold. Bricks had been placed in the oven to heat; they were now wrapped in carpet and put in the wagons to keep the guests' feet warm. It took most of them at least an hour and a half behind plodding horses to reach their homes.

FAMILY AND FRIENDS

After pursuing medical degrees in Boulder and New York, Homer James served the community of Alma, Colorado. He returned to Estes Park to run Elkhorn Lodge in 1895.
IMAGE COURTESY OF ESTES PARK MUSEUM. 2003.006.002-81

Homer

My eldest brother, Homer James, was a regular bookworm, and my parents decided that he was the one who should have the best education. He went to the University of Colorado and attended one of the first classes in medicine to be offered at the University. He was also on the first football team there.

After receiving his diploma in medicine, he went to New York City for post-graduate work at the New York Poly-Clinic. On his return to Colorado, a Dr. Toploff [sic] of Longmont offered him a position in his office, but Homer wanted to go where he was not known. He chose Alma, a mining town, the highest incorporated town in the United States at that time.

He was kept busy taking care of miners and their families, but he nearly starved to death. When Saturday came and the miners

Photo of Ella McCabe James, c. 1915. After her husband's death in 1895, Ella ran Elkhorn Lodge with the help of her children, Homer, Howard, and Eleanor. IMAGE COURTESY OF ESTES PARK MUSEUM. 1970.025.002-PG.90

FAMILY AND FRIENDS

The Estes Park Golf and Country Club was founded in 1918.
POSTCARD COURTESY OF R.A. HEISTERKAMP.

got their pay, they would take it to the saloons and gamble and drink it away.

After my father died, Mother sent for Homer to come back and manage Elkhorn Lodge. Howard, who was several years younger than Homer, was a born hotel man, but Mother seemed to think he was too young, so Homer took over.

He had a good deal of trouble with the help; if they were insubordinate, he would discharge them even though he might not know where he could replace them. Sometimes the same thing happened with the guests.

Homer was very fond of golf, and finally organized and established the Estes Park Country Club. One fall, he went into the pole patch and selected the logs for the clubhouse, and with the help of Ed Andrews, constructed the building and managed the country club for a couple of years.

Usually people were dead or dying before they sent for a doctor. At that time in Estes Park, we had but one doctor, and he spent a

FAMILY AND FRIENDS

good deal of time as a carpenter. So Homer's services were needed from time to time.

The first case I remember Homer having was the Swedish caretaker at the Crocker Ranch, who had a very bad cold. Homer told him to go to bed and stay there. The next day, when he called on his patient, he found the man had gone to bed, but had got up at five o'clock to milk the cow and feed the horse. He did this the following day, too. Homer finally had to go to the Crocker Ranch to nurse his patient and also to milk the cow and feed the horse. After about ten days of this routine, the man was well enough to take over.

The next case was of a woman in Horseshoe Park who had suffered a severe hemorrhage. Homer said she had to build up her blood, but he found she was eating tea and toast one day and toast and tea the next. It looked as though she might pass out of the picture.

This Mother and I could not stand, so we took over. I made quarts of beef tea. In case you do not know how to make beef tea, this is how it is done. Cut up pieces of beef, put them in a glass jar; put the jar in a pan of cold water, and place on the stove to boil. When thoroughly heated, take the pan off the stove, and put the meat through a press to squeeze out all of the juice.

At that time, we had a half a beef hanging in the meat house; I am unable to say how much of that animal I made into beef tea.

Mother's contribution was port wine; the woman drank all of Mother's port wine, and eventually was pronounced out of danger. Homer got the credit, but I always thought Mother and I deserved it.

One day, Mrs. Carlyle Lamb came down from Longs Peak Inn with a badly ulcerated tooth and asked my brother to pull it. When he advanced toward her with the forceps, she backed away. Finally, he gave her a stiff drink of brandy. Lo and behold, the tooth stopped aching. Mrs. Lamb went home, only to appear the next day in abject misery. She begged Homer to give her some more of that "good medicine," which he did. A second time she lost her courage and went back to the Inn. The third day when she appeared, Homer put

FAMILY AND FRIENDS

Howard James

her in a chair. He got her mouth open, and he pulled a tooth, but he was never quite sure whether or not it was the right one.

He never got paid for his services, because he never presented a bill.

Howard and Mother

After my brother Howard took over the management of Elkhorn Lodge and I had married and was tired of riding horseback and dancing, my husband and I lived at the Lodge. I begged Howard to let me help him in the office. Mother was delighted with this arrangement; Howard did not think it would last.

My Mother had given many years of her life helping to establish Elkhorn, and now was chatting with the guests and helping to entertain them. There was not a day she did not read her Bible. On Sunday, we found she was gathering up the billiard and pool balls and hiding them because she considered it too noisy a game to be played on Sunday. She thoroughly enjoyed playing cards, but not for money.

One summer, we had a group of people, twelve in all, who played "500" every night. Each one contributed ten cents, and at the end of the evening there was a first and second prize of the money contributed.

Ella James and her son Howard.

Mother said, "Ella, those people play cards every night. I wish they would ask me to play with them."

"Why, Mother," I replied, "they play for money."

One evening I was asked to fill in for one of the players who had a sick headache or had gone to the movies.

"If you will let me play until Mother comes, I will be very happy to turn my hand over to her," I told them. To this they agreed.

I had a very good start; when Mother arrived, she carried on. At the end of the evening, I met her coming across the living room with a handful of dimes.

"Why, Mother," I teased, "you've been playing for money!"

"Oh, no, I haven't," she replied. "This is the prize!"

We often bought fresh peas from Mr. Alexander Boyd who lived in Morraine [sic] Park. It was very hard to get the cooks in the kitchen to shell the fresh peas; they much preferred to open tin cans.

So mother would arrange herself on the front porch, have a basket of peas brought to her with some pans, and start to shell peas. In no time, there would be nine or ten people sitting around her,

FAMILY AND FRIENDS

Mother's picnic

shelling peas like mad, while Mother entertained them with tales of her pioneer days.

When my Father died, he left everything to Mother. From time to time, we would build a large addition to the Lodge, and of course would have to borrow money. Then Mother would make us stay in the Park winter as well as summer until the money was paid back, because she said it did not belong to her.

Every year we gave a picnic for Mother. This was not an ordinary picnic when we sat upon the ground or on logs, but an "affair." We set out card tables and folding chairs in a shady spot, and there was considerable thought given to the menu. Mother invited her own guests, and sometimes she would have as many as fifty or sixty people.

There is one little picture I hope to include of two little old ladies sitting side by side. One was Mother and the other Mrs. Sprague— Abner Sprague's mother, one of the early settlers.

My brother Howard was devoted to Mother. On Sunday, which was a busy day at Elkhorn, he would drive her to church, go about

Howard James with his mother, Mrs W. E. (Ella McCabe) James.
IMAGE COURTESY OF ESTES PARK MUSEUM. 1985.063.289

FAMILY AND FRIENDS

his errands, but would always be there when church let out to bring Mother home.

I've often heard Mother brag to other people about how fond the guests were of Howard. "The women all kiss him goodbye when they leave," she would say. Mother died at the age of seventy-four.

⌇

Late one summer, a bear killed one of the steers in Horseshoe Park, so Howard set out the bear trap. The next day he rode in to report that the bear was in the trap.

The trap was on a long chain, which ended in a large ring. A long pole was placed through the ring. This arrangement allowed the bear to move about, but the dragging pole prevented his escape. Had the trap been secured, the bear might have chewed off his leg in his agony and fear and his attempt to get away.

Almost everyone at the Lodge decided to go out to see the bear. It was before the days of automobiles, so we went on horseback or in wagons. When we arrived at Horseshoe Lake, we could hear the bear threshing around in the underbrush at the other side of the lake.

I decided that the thing to do was to go up the hill; then I could look down and see the bear. I topped a small rise and to my horror discovered that the bear was only about thirty yards from me. The log was dragging and catching now and then in the brush, but I feared he might attack me. I tried to walk away, but was so frightened I couldn't move. A young man saw my dilemma, came up to me and led me down the hill past the bear.

Ahead of us were a Mr. and Mrs. G., struggling through the bogholes and brush in their haste to get away from the bear and back to the wagon. He was a big, tall, thin man; she was a short fat woman, and she had a firm grip on her husband's arm.

Then she tripped and fell on her face. Her husband shook her off and hurried on without her. The young man who had rescued me helped Mrs. G. to her feet and escorted her back to the wagon.

43

There in the front seat sat the man who had vowed to love and protect her all the days of his life!

(I've often thought marriage vows should be altered from time to time; I think the word "obey" could safely be omitted.)

About this time, Howard appeared with his gun. A bear has a very thick skull, and has to be shot in the eye or a vulnerable spot in the chest. It took about eight shots to kill this one. Eventually, the skin was sent to Denver, where the head was mounted and the skin was lined. It reposes now on the wall of the living room at Elkhorn.

The following story always makes me shiver. From our winter home in Longmont, Howard had returned to the Park to oversee the filling of the ice-house. He stayed alone at the Lodge, and one evening about eleven o'clock was lying on the couch in the living room. It was a bright moonlight night, and there was a lot of snow on the ground.

Howard heard an animal step up onto the porch and walk slowly toward the window near the couch where he was lying. He realized it was a large animal by the sound of its tread in the snow on the porch. He lay there listening as the animal came closer and closer. Suddenly, he found himself looking into the eyes of a mountain lion.

The man and the lion stared at each other. (Howard said it seemed like a half an hour, but it was probably not more than a minute or two.)

Howard jumped off the couch; at the same time, the lion leaped from the porch and ran off down toward the river. Howard got his rifle, then decided that eleven o'clock on a moonlight night was no time to go lion hunting. By the next morning, all tracks had been obliterated by blowing snow.

In the spring of 1927, Mr. Hondius went to Holland for the summer. Florine Townsend, my room clerk, young Pieter, and I joined him

FAMILY AND FRIENDS

Pieter and Eleanor Hondius with Pieter, Jr., on Waikiki Beach, Honolulu, Hawaii, c. 1925. IMAGE COURTESY OF ESTES PARK MUSEUM.

in the fall. Not having a visa for Holland, we could stay there only eight days; from there we went to Italy, where we spent about two months.

Then Mr. Hondius wanted to see Egypt; we found it very cold, so decided to go on to our beloved Honolulu in the Hawaiian Islands. Young Pieter celebrated his fifth birthday aboard ship in the Indian Ocean.

It was the first part of May, 1928, when we got back to Estes Park. There we found Howard very sick; he lived only about a month after our return.

Then it was a good thing I had my earlier training at Elkhorn Lodge, for now I had to manage it by myself.

That first summer I always tried to forget. I knew so little about Howard's part of the work! How I ever lived through that first summer, I'll never know. The following spring, I went to Phoenix

FAMILY AND FRIENDS

In 1914, Roger Toll (hatless, at left) accompanied the Indian representatives identifying Arapahoe sites in the Estes Valley.
IMAGE COURTESY OF ESTES PARK MUSEUM. 1984.036.018.

and persuaded Charles Doak, chef at the Phoenix Biltmore, and his wife Margaret, to join the staff at Elkhorn. From that time on, at least we had good food.

Always on Sunday, we served the famous Elkhorn cream pie; Sunday night, there was cornmeal mush, beefsteak, and Welsh rarebit. To this day, people go to the Lodge hoping to get the beefsteak and Welsh rarebit on Sunday night.

No matter where I was during the winter, I had to return to Elkhorn by the first of April, and Ella Kramer, my wonderful housekeeper who was with me for twenty-seven years, engaged her girls for housekeeping.

Many things I had to order before the steward came. I learned to order hundreds of cases of eggs, which were put in the Beatrice Creamery for storage. Fresh eggs for the table were provided by farmers in the valley with whom I had to negotiate contracts. I ordered sacks of potatoes from Idaho for baking; they had to measure a certain size. We bought our meat from Swift Packing Co., and every spring I went through the packing plant to order loins

Studio photos of Eleanor and Pieter Hondius.

of beef for roasts and steaks; these had to be hung in the freezing unit for several months.

After the hotel opened, which was usually about the first of June, I had a steward who took charge of the storeroom. Salesmen from the wholesale houses would come to him each day for their orders.

Pieter Hondius

After Howard died, my husband was a great comfort to me, although he had nothing to do with the management of the Lodge. I would like to tell you something about this nice husband of mine.

He was a Hollander by birth, but after he came to America at twenty-seven, he became a naturalized citizen. Mr. Hondius came from a long line of distinguished ancestors—men of letters and artists, among them the famous fifteenth- and sixteenth-century cardiographer, Jon Jacobus Puppius Hondius [sic]. In the Huntington Library in Pasadena, California, are two huge globes made by him, one celestial, the other terrestrial, and also many of his maps. Mr. Hondius bought for Pieter a Hondius atlas from a Jewish antique dealer in Amsterdam that dated back to the Sixteenth Century.

The Hondius coat of arms.

Pieter Hondius as a young man.
IMAGE COURTESY OF ESTES PARK MUSEUM. 1985.063.296

One of his family was sainted, St. Conesius [sic], whose given name was Pieter deHondt. This ancestor was a minister in the court of Austria at the time of the Spanish Inquisition in Holland. Pieter deHondt, a Catholic, carried out an Inquisition all his own in Austria, and many years later he was cannonized. Mr. Hondius's father, being a direct descendent, was invited to the ceremonies. He refused because he was a strict member of the Dutch Reformed Church.

Pieter often said, "We don't have to worry about getting into Heaven. If Gabriel isn't there to welcome us, there will be St. Conesius."

When Mr. Hondius was three years old, he developed asthma. His father took him to Lake Lucerne in Switzerland, where they stayed for a year, hoping Pieter would outgrow the attack. However, because Holland is such a wet country, he had constantly to go back to Switzerland. Finally the Doctor told him he would have to live in Switzerland the year around, or go to the mountains of North America or he would have emphysema of the lungs.

He chose to come to Denver. He did not want to stay in the city, so Dr. Rudi [sic], a Swiss doctor, recommended that he go to Estes

FAMILY AND FRIENDS

Park. Like all others after the season was over, he was deposited at our door.

He bought something like 2,000 acres of land in the Park, and decided to go into the cattle business, but he did not reckon with ragweed and timothy, which gave him hay fever and eventually attacks of asthma. Then he would have to change altitude and go either to timberline on a camping trip or to Denver.

The ranch on which he lived was known as the Beaver. One year Miss Vail [*sic*], a cousin of Mr. Roger Tolle [*sic*], paid the expenses of two Indians who came to the Park to verify that they had been there years before. One was supposed to have lived in the Park when he was sixteen, another at the age of eight; a third Indian in the party served as interpreter. They made camp on the Beaver; Shep Husted kept the camp for them and served as cook and horse wrangler. He told me this story:

> *These Indians claimed that there was a huge tree high on the side of Deer Mountain by a spring. A woman of their tribe, ill with a skin disease; had been left under this tree with food and camping facilities for a month. When the tribe returned, she was dead. So they called the valley "Al-sa-de-non-tok" which means "The valley where the woman died."*

Mr. Hondius could not remember the big tree they described, although he knew about the spring, which he used for his pipeline. So one day, while the Indians were there, Mr. Hondius climbed the mountain and found near the spring the remains of a huge tree stump. Then he believed that the Indians were telling the truth.

The people of Estes Park do not seem to know this valley by any other name than the Beaver. Mr. Hondius finally sold his land to the government, and it became part of Rocky Mountain National Park.

⤳

Because of his health, Mr. Hondius went to Arizona in the winter, and after little Pieter came, we spent every other winter in Hawaii.

49

FAMILY AND FRIENDS

Pieter, Jr., and his father

Even then, the dampness was too much; Mr. Hondius finally sold and settled in Palm Springs, California, where he died in 1934.

My Son

Pieter was eleven years old when his father died; and although he has grown into a fine man, of whom I am very proud, still there were many times when he needed his wonderful father.

For a few years, he played with the guests' children during the summer, and they spent most of their time around the stables. Gradually, Pieter was acquiring a vocabulary I did not care for.

I was therefore delighted when Mr. McCreery, who owned a dairy, wrote to Pieter offering him a summer job. Pieter was then about fifteen and attending Fountain Valley School in Colorado Springs.

Mr. McCreery gave me the reply he received from Pieter. It went something like this: "Dear Mr. McCreery, Thank you so much for offering me a position. I have never milked a cow, but I see no

FAMILY AND FRIENDS

Studio photo of Pieter Hondius, Jr., in his cowboy outfit, c. 1929.

reason I cannot learn if I try hard enough." It was understood that Pieter would have two days a week at Elkhorn.

One Sunday morning during this summer, Mr. Talley, one of the guests at Elkhorn, returned from church and said to me, "Mrs. Hondius, I saw a beautiful sight this morning."

"What was that?" I asked.

"Young Pieter ushering at church," he replied.

Throughout the years at Elkhorn, summer Sundays were so busy I seldom got to church, but Pieter attended Sunday School regularly. I did not know he had assumed the role of an usher at church until Mr. Talley told me about it, but from then on, each summer in Estes Park found him also serving as a church usher on Sundays.

Another summer he was a grease monkey with Johnny Bill Ramey in the village. Most of the grease drained from the cars, he

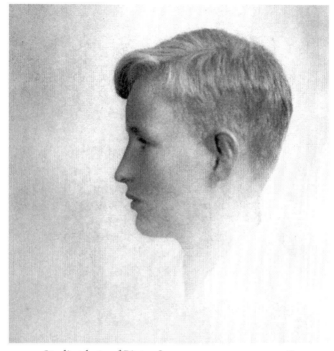

Studio photo of Pieter, Jr., as a young man, c. 1938.

seemed to bring home on his clothes, and I was very glad when that job was over. Then for two or three summers he was delivery boy for K & B Packing Co. in the village.

I encouraged this work because it was so much better for him to have something to do than to spend his time riding horseback, and as I have said before, acquiring a new vocabulary.

After he finished high school, he entered the NROTC program at the University of Colorado. He would not wait until he got his commission, however, but insisted on enlisting. He said he had not felt like a man for a year.

He went into the Navy, assigned to radar and sonar section of the flagship of a group of L.S.T.s, and was sent to the South Pacific. When his tour of duty was completed, I asked him what he wanted to do.

FAMILY AND FRIENDS

Studio photo of Pieter, Jr., as an adult, c. 1945.

"I'm going back to the University and get a degree," he replied. "Without an education, you get nowhere in this world."

He spent two summers and three winters at the University before his graduation, and joined Delta Tau Delta fraternity. During the summer he was not at the University, he was employed by Mr. Earl Carmack, who was head mechanic of the National Park Service. That summer a group of men were sent up to the top of Flattop Mountain, working on the telephone system.

Some of the men were thirty-five and forty years of age, and when I asked Pieter why Mr. Carmack trusted the overseeing of this work to him, he said, "Because he knows I'm his friend, and he trusts me."

The Pipeline

When he had discontinued his ranching, Mr. Hondius built a pipeline that extended six miles from the upper part of the Beaver, with

Johnny Adams's original cabin.
IMAGE COURTESY OF ESTES PARK MUSEUM. 1980.036.004.

reservoirs all along the way to store the water when not in use. This pipeline I inherited.

I had to furnish water to 150 summer cottages from the first of May to the first of October. The contract stated that if "by act of God" there was not sufficient snow on the range or rain during the summer to supply the creeks and springs with water, and I had used all diligence to keep the line clean and in use, I could not be held responsible.

The people who owned the cottages were not to use the water for anything except household purposes. There was scarcely one of them, however, who did not transplant a lot of little trees or shrubs and try to raise a lawn. Johnny Adams took care of the pipeline for me, and several times at ten or eleven o'clock at night, I would have to go get Johnny and take him to the Beaver to run down the person or persons who were draining our pipeline.

There was one woman in particular who had a whole hillside of flowers. When I remonstrated with her and threatened to turn the water off, she retorted, "If you had been living right, the Lord would have given you all the water you needed."

Johnny Adams

Johnny Adams at eighteen was a stableboy at Elkhorn Lodge; in his twenties he took up land about four miles above the Lodge on the Fall River. He was a quiet man, a kind man, and an incessant reader.

Johnny walked back and forth to the village for his supplies and newspapers. Although he was no ladies' man, Mrs. Hayden or Miss Gookin would often drive him back to his ranch from the village. Mrs. Stanley one time invited Johnny to dinner at her home. She was curious to know how he would act in a formal drawing room. A few days afterward I asked her about the dinner. "Mr. Adams was just the same in my drawing room as when I talk to him in the village," she replied. I have always thought that gentlemen are born and not made, and Johnny was a gentleman.

Whenever Mr. Hondius was lonely or restless, he would go to the village, buy a basket of grapes or a bag of peanuts, go get Johnny, and the two of them would spend the day together. Although Mr. Hondius was a highly educated man, and Johnny had little formal education, the two were fast friends and had much in common.

Before his death, Mr. Hondius stated that he wished to leave Johnny a few hundred dollars in his will so that Johnny could buy some books or something to remember him by. "I just want to express somehow my admiration and respect for him," Mr. Hondius said.

I always had to come back to Estes Park by the first of April, and one year I found that Johnny had sold his land to George McGrew. He had kept two acres on which there was a spring, and had built a new cottage, which consisted of a living room, kitchen, and screened-in utility porch. Stanny and Rita Jones [sic], the wives of two of Johnny's close friends, had made curtains for the windows of the new home.

Johnny Adams' "new cottage," which his friends and neighbors helped to furnish. IMAGE COURTESY OF ESTES PARK MUSEUM. 1980.036.002

I had given only one "shower," and that was for a bride-to-be. I thought it would be a good idea to give a shower for Johnny Adams, a bachelor, although I had some trouble persuading him that it was the thing to do.

Mrs. McDonald gave a kitchen sink, and Mr. Jones, the plumber, installed it for Johnny. He had it placed so high on the wall that some of us teased him about using it for a shower bath.

We put linoleum on the kitchen floor, got dishes and cutlery and cooking utensils, and a kitchen table and chairs. In the living room, Johnny had a brand new bed with innerspring mattress; of course this bed had to have blankets and linen. We had enough money to buy a new chair or two, and a table for his books.

We dressed Johnny's cabin up so nicely we decided to do away with the housewarming for fear some designing woman might try to acquire Johnny and his new abode, and undo all the good we had tried to do for him.

Johnny continued to take care of my pipeline for me. During the winter, he lived with friends in Boulder. He had had an operation performed by a Ft. Collins doctor, and many times he would have to consult this doctor. Pieter, who was in school at the University, drove Johnny to Ft. Collins to see the doctor on many Saturdays.

When Johnny died, Pieter was asked to be one of the pall bearers. Pieter was in his early twenties; the rest of the pall bearers were at least fifty years old. The church was filled with people and flowers. That afternoon, on our way up the Park hill, Pieter said to me, "I think Johnny was the best man I ever knew."

This was a last tribute he paid to his friend.

Community Work

The Estes Park Protective and Improvement Association was formed in September, 1906, with Mr. Stanley as president and Mr. C. H. Bond as secretary.

The Association's aim was the development of the Park through publicity, the building of roads and trails, the establishment and maintenance of a fish hatchery, the enforcement of the game laws, and the protection of wild flowers.

Most property owners at once became members. As a result, a fish hatchery, which has placed several million young trout in neighboring streams, was built and maintained.

The money for the hatchery was contributed by a group of men; each year, it was quite a struggle to get the necessary funds. For a time it looked as though they might have to abandon it.

Then the women took over. They gave bazaars, dances, candy sales, and for many years maintained the fish hatchery. The women's

FAMILY AND FRIENDS

Studio portrait of Eleanor Estes James Hondius, c. 1910.
IMAGE COURTESY OF ESTES PARK MUSEUM. 1985.063.329

group was known as the Auxiliary to the Estes Park Improvement and Protective Association.

Finally, the State took over the hatchery. That summer, we decided to raise money for roads and trails; and because a group of men in the community known as the Businessmen's Association had the same goal, we combined forces and held a dance every two weeks at a different hotel.

I went to the last meeting of the Protective Society to hand over the $300 to $400 we had raised that summer. I was told it was kind of us to have raised the money, but we were only an Auxiliary, and could not dictate to the Association the use of the money. I refused to hand over the money.

A few weeks later, the women met at the Hupp Hotel and formed a society known as the Women's [sic] Club, which has been in existence since. The money went into our own treasury.

⤷

The women held bazaars, dances and candy sales at the different hotels. A couple of times we had a circus tent sent up from Denver, which was put up in the Park by the library. Of course, we had a tea room, a candy table, a raffle booth, and always Mrs. Stanley would come dressed as a gypsy and tell fortunes by the reading of palms and with cards. It was surprising how much money these bazaars, dances, and candy sales made.

I remember one booth we had. It was a handkerchief booth, and the girls who had charge of it sent invitations to all the prominent people they could think of, stating that we had to feed the "little fitches."

The first handkerchief to arrive was one from the White House, sent by Mrs. Herbert Hoover, who was then our First Lady. Another came from Admiral Peary, who discovered the North Pole. It was a wreck of a handkerchief, all covered with ink. The only thing that made it worthwhile was the sarcastic letter from the Admiral that accompanied it. I can't remember who all contributed, but we made more money on the sale of the letters than from the sale of the handkerchiefs.

⤷

FAMILY AND FRIENDS

One of the last bazaars given by the Woman's Club was held at Elkhorn. It started at ten in the morning, and it was midnight before it ended. Mrs. Hollebird [sic] of Chicago had charge of the tea room, which was set up in the card room. I always had charge of the candy table. Then we had dancing in the ballroom, and many things throughout the Lodge, such as books of souvenir pictures of the Park, raffles, and of course, Mrs. Stanley telling fortunes.

There was a table of fancywork, and many other things I have forgotten. I know that we took in $1300, but $400 of that was expense. So in the end, we turned over $900 to the library.

I must add that there was a man from Chicago who taught my Uncle John, a good Methodist, how to make a roulette table. It was a surprise to everyone, but it brought us an additional $80. We used it for two years, until the Woman's Club decided it was wicked.

Uncle John

My Uncle John was quite a character. He came to the Lodge every summer and made himself useful. People who had lost the keys to their trunks called on Uncle John to unlock them. In fact, we always called him "Mr. Fixit."

At one time while Pieter was a little boy, he had a very runny nose, which we seemed unable to control and which gave us a lot of trouble. I asked, "What will we do with your nose?" He replied, "Get Uncle John to fix it!"

Uncle John was at least eighty years old and had a long curly white beard which he adored, constantly stroking it. I tried to persuade him to let me trim it a bit, and one day he consented. I'm afraid I took advantage, and trimmed too much, for Uncle John had to go to the barber and came out with a lovely VanDyke.

In the middle of the summer, he always had a birthday, and everybody made an occasion of that. When Uncle John appeared in his Sunday best on a weekday, we knew we had forgotten again that it was his birthday.

FAMILY AND FRIENDS

Piles of elk antlers like this one were the hotel's signature, and marked the entrance to Elkhorn Lodge from early times.
IMAGE COURTESY OF ESTES PARK MUSEUM. 2006.006.005_19

Some of the guests would arrange a game of golf, and then there was a big dinner for Uncle John, with a big birthday cake. Because he liked cigars but never bought any for himself, he would receive boxes of cigars through the mail. People who remembered his birthday better than we did would write birthday greetings.

After Uncle John had blown out the candles on his cake and had sent pieces of the cake here and there to different friends in the dining room, everyone would stand up and sing, "Happy birthday, Uncle John; happy birthday to you!" Uncle John would make a bow and depart with what was left of his birthday cake, which he divided among the chambermaids.

Ralph Gwin [*sic*], who owned the motion picture theater, gave Uncle John a season pass so that he could take another person with him when he went to the movies. But finally he had to give him another pass, because Uncle John always had to take two girls instead of one. It seemed that there was safety in numbers. Uncle John, at eighty, was sometimes too affectionate.

CHAPTER SIX

Entertainment at Elkhorn

We usually opened the Lodge for the season on Decoration Day. June was a slow month, although we could always depend on stenographers and brides and grooms as guests during that month.

I remember one case especially. A young couple came to the Lodge, and of course we knew they had just been newly wed.

The next day, the clerk came to me and said, "Mrs. Hondius, I think we need a little help. Remember that young couple that came in yesterday? The boy came to me and said, 'My wife is homesick and wants to go right home. This is supposed to be our honeymoon, and we were to be away two weeks. I don't know what to do about it.'"

With that, we got busy. We took them horseback riding in the daytime, gave them beefsteak fries in the evening, and took them to Riverside

ENTERTAINMENT AT ELKHORN

Eleanor E. Hondius.

for dancing. In two or three days, we had a happy bride. When they left, they told us what a wonderful time they had had.

It was not so hard to entertain the stenographers. All I had to do was to find plenty of beaus for them for the evening.

One year a Mr. and Mrs. Flagg of New York City and their three daughters came to spend the summer at Elkhorn. They rented the Pauley cottage across the river from Elkhorn, and took their meals at the Lodge. Mr. Flagg was not well, and he had come to Estes Park for his health.

Summer guests departing Elkhorn Lodge in a Stanley Steam car, c. 1910. IMAGE COURTESY OF ESTES PARK MUSEUM. 1984.036.024.

At that time, we had three or four unattached men staying at Elkhorn, who asked me to introduce them to the girls. Very few of our guests came from the East Coast, so I had to feel my way about introductions. I told Mrs. Flagg these young men would like to meet her daughters; would she allow me to introduce them? She, in turn, asked if I knew anything about them.

"No," I answered, "but they seem very nice, and pay their bills." (I found out afterward that one of these young men was married and had three or four children.)

Mrs. Flagg said, "My daughters are women of the world and can take care of themselves, so it will be all right."

They certainly did know how to take care of themselves! The three girls rode horseback nearly every day, and as extra boys appeared, they would appropriate them. They were not so generous about including the girls. One thing they enjoyed very much was having a private beefsteak fry in the evening, and many nights at eight or nine o'clock we would hear their horses running up the road. A half hour later, we would hear a slow "carump-carump-carump" and we knew it was Mrs. Flagg on her mama horse, for

ENTERTAINMENT AT ELKHORN

In a snapshot taken in August 1900, Eleanor James (right front) joins Elkhorn Lodge guests enjoying watermelon slices.
IMAGE COURTESY OF ESTES PARK MUSEUM. 2006.006.004_91

she always chaperoned her daughters. They started out together, but they never returned home together.

One summer we had an Admiral Winslow and his family; his wife, the former Miss Havermire [sic] of New York, two teenage sons, three daughters, and a lady's maid. The Winslows were from Boston; Elkhorn had been recommended to them as a place where they would get good food and have a nice time. Mrs. Winslow always went back to her cottage after meals; but the Admiral and the rest of the family took part in what was going on. The Admiral was seventy-four years old, and loved to play tennis.

The following summer, they came again; this time they had the home cottage across the river, and brought a second maid, who prepared their breakfasts. They took the rest of their meals at

ENTERTAINMENT AT ELKHORN

Elkhorn. Mrs. Winslow had never drawn a bath in her life, but one day at the cottage decided to do so. She turned on the hot water, which was practically boiling, filled the tub, and then had to wait until it cooled enough to take her bath. They complained about not having enough hot water, but the cottage had an eighty-four-gallon tank, and the fireman certainly kept the water hot.

That fall I wrote asking if they would like the cottage the following summer. The Admiral answered, saying he was sorry, they were afraid to risk another summer. They had three marriageable daughters who must marry among their own class. They previously had gone to their house in Newport for the summer, with a staff of sixteen people to take care of them. He stated that he and his wife had such a wonderful rest those two summers at Elkhorn. I subscribed to "Town and Country," and would occasionally read of the family's gay times in Newport.

We did a great deal to entertain the guests at Elkhorn. Usually Friday noon, my brother Howard would have a fish fry four or five miles up the river; on Wednesday night, we usually had a beefsteak fry. After I came into the office, I started the breakfast rides. I would have to make up a list of the people who would ride their horses or drive their cars about four miles to the picnic grounds. It was quite a task to get some of them up, and I would have to send a porter two or three times to knock on their doors before they appeared.

On Sunday we usually had a lecture or a musicale. These entertainers always had to be introduced. I will never forget the time I introduced Dr. Stone, who was known and loved by everyone anyway. When the time came, the boys had to hunt for me; I was out at the woodpile trying to persuade two waitresses to change their plans about leaving the next day. I finally assured them that we could not run the Lodge without them.

ENTERTAINMENT AT ELKHORN

Then one night, the naturalist from the National Park Service came. In the spring, I had known her as Dr. Fuller; but shortly thereafter, she had married a man by the name of Booze [sic]. So I said, "Ladies and gentlemen, I have a great treat in store for you this evening. The National Park naturalist, Dr. Fuller Booze, will talk to us about the birds, the bees, and the flowers!"

The Woman's Club of Estes Park always had an entertainment at two or three hotels during the summer, and each of us had to provide our own entertainers. Appearing on the Elkhorn program one summer was a Mr. Garardi, a member of the Boston Symphony, who was visiting Mr. and Mrs. Stanley. Then there was a Miss Polk, who had a beautiful voice, and had consented to sing for us; and a Mr. David Geon of Texas, who was going to play some of his own compositions.

We had to wait for the reader who was coming from the Fall River Lodge; she had to wash the noon dishes before she could come. It was a hectic day for me. The entertainment was given in the living room; the chairs had to be moved from the dining room as soon as they were vacated. Then I had to get the punch bowl, the punch, and the wafers ready. In fact, I doubt if I had time to wash my face.

Then Mr. Garardi said, "How are you going to introduce me?"

I said, "Mr. Garardi of the Boston Symphony has consented to play for us this afternoon."

"Oh, no," he protested. "You must say I am the youngest member of the violin section of the Symphony."

Next Miss Polk asked me how I was going to introduce Mr. Geon [sic]. I told her; it did not meet with her approval. When the time came, I tried to keep in mind her instructions, which included the information that Mr. Geon was known in this country and in Europe as the greatest composer of Negro Spirituals.

67

ENTERTAINMENT AT ELKHORN

Trail rides were popular activities at the Elkhorn, and gymkhana games were a part of the summer season.
IMAGE COURTESY OF ESTES PARK MUSEUM, C. 1915. 1987.058.004

Mr. Geon was the last number on the program, and I said, "Ladies and gentlemen, I have a great treat in store for you this afternoon. Mr. David Geon of Texas will play some of his own compositions for you. Mr. Geon is known not only in this country but in Europe as the greatest Negro spiritualist."

The audience laughed, and so did I. Poor Mr. Geon didn't see anything funny about it.

Those summers when people had to be introduced, I learned that the principal artist was the last on the program. We had a guest at the Lodge who had a very beautiful voice, and one Sunday she said she would sing. The other music was to be furnished by our trio: piano, violin, and cello.

Then Emily McGew who lived in the Park persuaded her sister-in-law who was visiting her to appear on the program. Rose McGrew had lived many years abroad, and had sung in the German Grand Opera for the Kaiser Wilhelm.

ENTERTAINMENT AT ELKHORN

Summer entertainments at the Elkhorn Lodge included musical evenings and amateur theatricals. The bunting hanging over the heads of this group of players suggests a July 4th program.
IMAGE COURTESY OF ESTES PARK MUSEUM. 2003.006.001-29.

When the evening arrived, she certainly fulfilled all Mrs. McGrew had said about her; she had a magnificent voice, and sang in German, Italian and French. Her finale, in English, was a simple song, "The End of a Perfect Day."

I knew I was in trouble with my guest, so I hid out. The next day, I had to apologize and eat humble pie.

There was something doing almost all the time at Elkhorn. Sometimes we would have bridge tournaments, where the guests selected their own partners and drew their opponents. It is very difficult to play bridge unless you have good cards to play with, and consequently, sometimes the best players would be eliminated

ENTERTAINMENT AT ELKHORN

in the first round. These tournaments would last three or four days; each player contributed about fifty cents or a dollar, and at the end of the tournament there was a nice purse for the winners.

One summer a Mr. and Mrs. X from Chicago stayed at the Lodge for about two months. They did not play cards, nor ride horseback. They really didn't have a very gay time.

Finally, Mrs. X decided to contribute something to the summer season and wanted to have a flower show. She asked me what I thought of the idea. Secretly, I didn't think much of it, but I said I would put a notice on the dining-room door announcing the flower show, and asking anyone who wishes to enter the contest to leave his name at the desk.

Every day for several days, Mrs. X came to find out how the list was growing. It wasn't. So I offered to do what I could to help her. As well as the notice, I was at the dining-room door, too, and any-one who went through I coaxed and entreated until I finally added his or her name as flower show contestants.

Things were finally going very nicely in fact, I had to go out-side the lodge to borrow vases. One guest, who weighed about 200 pounds, picked flowers for several days before the show. In fact, I think she must have picked all of the flowers within a radius of two miles, because the day of the flower show, I met Mrs. Ida Wight and another woman coming back from the north end of the park, where they had gone to pick flowers.

"Hurry, now, or you'll miss your lunch," I called.

Mrs. Wight smiled and commented, "I hate you."

Well, the ballroom was very gay, bright with flower arrange-ments of all sizes and colors. The show had been well advertised, so we had plenty of people from outside the Lodge who came to see the show. Dr. Wood, I know, was one of the judges; possibly Mr. Pauley and Mr. Cox were the others.

Mr. and Mrs. X were greeting everyone, and it was really quite an affair. The winning entry of the show turned out to be a wicker basket with five or six purple thistles stuck in it.

ENTERTAINMENT AT ELKHORN

Entries in the Elkhorn Lodge's one and only flower show.
IMAGE COURTESY OF ESTES PARK MUSEUM. 1985.063.197

The next day, I had the pleasure of returning the vases and getting rid of the wilted flowers. I mentally resolved never to have another flower show.

        ~

For several years we had two machines at Elkhorn called "one-armed bandits." Into one, we fed five cent pieces; into the other, dimes. These machines belonged to a man who got 40% of the proceeds; Elkhorn got 40%, and the American Legion got 20%. Some places in the village had machines which took quarters, half-dollars, and even dollars; but I held the line at the dime machines.

Everybody had great fun playing the "one-armed bandits." Occasionally they would give you back a few coins, and after many hours of hard work, you were lucky if you "broke the bank."

I remember one summer a Denver woman came to the Lodge with some friends for lunch and started playing the "bandit." She used all her money, all the money her chauffeur had, all the money she could borrow from her friends. Like the man who came for dinner and stayed for breakfast, she came for lunch and stayed for dinner before her friends could get her away from the "one-armed bandit."

Another evening a group of about eighty people formed a line in the ballroom. On one side of the room was the nickel machine, on the other the dime machine. Each of the guests had a handful of ammunition. In turn, each put a coin in one of the machines [and] pulled the handle; if lucky, the player got a few coins back; if not, he moved on, and the player behind him tried his luck. This game lasted for about two hours, and never a "jackpot." The next day, the dime machine gave up its coin when it received the first dime of the day!

The jackpot would pay $36 in coins on the dime machine; $20 on the nickel machine.

After lunch, most of the guests went to their rooms for a siesta. We had one guest who chose this time to play the "bandits." He would spend the entire afternoon hard at work. Every little while I would have to send a boy to the village to get more "ammunition."

One day, he came to the desk for another roll of dimes just as a second guest came in to see if the mail had arrived. The newcomer put his hand in his pocket, drew forth a dime, put it in the machine, pulled the lever—and hit the jackpot!

Money flew all over the floor. "That was my bank you broke!" shouted Player No. 1.

"It was my dime," retorted Guest No. 2.

I have never heard two little boys quarrel more violently than those two millionaires did over that $36 jackpot. I made my escape to the back office, not wanting to be called as referee.

We always had more young people at Elkhorn than any other two hotels in the Park. Once or twice during the summer, we entertained them at a dinner dance. The tables of the other guests would be pushed to the sides of the dining room, and down the middle of the room we would set up a long table—sometimes seating as many as 80 people.

We always had more girls than boys; I would have to go hunting for blind dates. George Storer, Channing Sweep [sic], Courtney Davis, William Allen White, Jr. [sic], one or two of the Hyde boys, and others I can't remember, were among these boys. If I did not have enough blind dates I could always call on the young rangers from the National Park. Of course, we always gave them a good dinner, furnished good music, and the girls were lovely in their evening dresses.

These dinner dances were very popular. Sometimes we took over the Country Club for them.

Another thing we used to have was a paper chase on horseback, patterned after "Hare and Hounds." This event was never popular with the livery men, because it was hard on the horses.

For at least a week before the paper chase, we collected newspapers, which were torn into small squares and put into bags. Two riders were chosen as "hares;" the day before the chase, they went out and planned the trail.

On the day of the chase, the "hares" were given about a half-hour head start, before the "hounds" started in pursuit.

Each of the "hares" carried a bag of torn-up newspapers; as they went along, they would scatter a handful of paper every twenty or thirty yards. They did everything to confuse the trail, throwing paper in rockpiles, doubling back on their trail. They rode about five or six miles, and then tied their horses in a grove of trees out of sight of the hounds. The first "hound" to find them won a prize, which was usually a purse of money made up by the paper chasers.

The hotel always sent out a picnic lunch to end the occasion. We never dared have more than one of these paper chases during the summer, because, as I have said, it was so hard on the horses.

Each year shortly before Frontier Days in Cheyenne, two busloads of Indians would come to Estes Park to dance at the Elkhorn, the Stanley, and in the village park. This, of course, was to advertise Frontier Days. I believe these Indians belonged to the Ute tribe, and only the men and young boys danced. The women stood

73

around in a circle and swayed from one foot to the other, while two or three beat on a sort of drum for the dancers to keep step by.

The guests assembled with cameras, taking pictures. When the Indians got tired of dancing, they would come up on the porch and appropriate the chairs until the buses came by to take them to their next engagement.

They always ate lunch and dinner at Elkhorn because we gave them more meat than any of the other places they had tried. Lunch and dinner were served in the ballroom, and the young daughters of the guests waited on the tables. This they considered great fun.

When lunch was ready, someone told the Chief, and the Indians would file down the porch to the side door of the ballroom. As each came in, he or she would shake hands with me and we would both say, "How!" One time, who should appear in the line but my son Pieter. We shook hands and said "How!" What prompted him to get in line with them I don't know.

These Indians were Christians, and they would not eat until they had said a blessing. One day, someone had put a quarter in the nickelodeon, which was making an uproar. The Indians refused to sit down to dinner. I couldn't imagine what the trouble was until one of the squaws [sic] came to me and said they could not say grace with that noise. Because the money had not been exhausted, the only thing I could do to stop the music was to pull the plug from the wall.

The Indians were always served big dishes of ice cream for dessert. Once two of the young girls collided and lost all the ice cream from their trays in a heap on the floor. The distress on the faces of those Indians astonished me. It was not until I assured them there was more ice cream in the kitchen that they found anything funny in the incident and could smile about it.

Sunday afternoon, instead of being a period of rest, was more like a Wild West show. Sometimes we had a baseball game in which

ENTERTAINMENT AT ELKHORN

Guests played a variety of games in front of the new Lodge building. In this snapshot a baseball game is underway.
IMAGE COURTESY OF ESTES PARK MUSEUM. 2003.006.001-29.

the guests played against the employees; but as a rule, the afternoon was devoted to bucking horses.

The guests would all be seated on the porches around the circle; cars coming up the highway would drive in, so we had a grandstand at the end of the grounds.

Sometimes we had gymkhana games on horseback; I can only remember two of these. One was musical chairs. We would pull the little piano from the ballroom at the end of the porch; the boys who took part in the game would ride their horses around the chairs. When the music stopped, they would fall off their horses and scramble for the chairs. There was always one more rider than there were chairs; the rider who did not get a chair was eliminated from the game. Each time the music started, a chair would be removed, and eventually only two riders would be circling about. There was always a purse for the winner.

The other gymkhana event was the garment race. Each contestant would be given a bag with some garment in it. They would

ENTERTAINMENT AT ELKHORN

race their horses from the starting point to the end of the grounds, dismount, open the bag, take out the garment, put it on, get back on their horses, and race back to the starting line. Sometimes the garment was a corset, or an old nightgown, or a blouse—anything hard to get into.

While the riders were struggling into the garments, usually the horses would get away and start back to the barn. But there was always someone ready to catch them and bring them back. This was a very amusing spectacle. There were other things they did in the gymkhana games, but these stand out in my memory.

One Sunday, Harry Lovern, the barnman, decided to make the afternoon really interesting. He put a blanket with a surcingle on a horse he felt certain would buck if spurred, and got one of his barnmen to ride the animal. There were a great many people watching this performance, automobiles all across in front of the hotel, guests on their porches. What no one knew was that Harry Lovern had fastened spurs to the blanket.

The horse did not disappoint anyone; it bucked furiously when touched by the spurs on the blanket. The poor rider clung to its back, although it seemed that at any moment he must be thrown. The horse, in its frenzy, began bucking close to the cars, and then decided to come up on the porch. Spectators scattered, hiding behind chairs, or seeking refuge where they could. The horse brushed against one of the posts on the porch, and knocked the boy off sideways. Fortunately, his feet came out of his boots. The horse went down between the cars, bucking his way to the barn.

Men ran to pick up the boy, who was apparently lifeless. They called for the doctor. Dr. Reed [sic], our house physician, reported that someone had taken his car and he had no way to get to the Lodge unless someone came for him. One of the guests, a young man who had a big Cadillac, said he would go if someone would show him where Dr. Reed's office was. I volunteered. It was a ride I'll never forget.

76

ENTERTAINMENT AT ELKHORN

Mr. and Mrs. Morris J. Bissell, parents of Mrs. Eleanor Reed [sic] of the Golden Horse Ranch, and others, in a 1910 Peerless auto in front of Elkhorn Lodge.

To my astonishment, the car had a siren like an ambulance, and every now and then, a gong would sound. We went toward the village at a terrific rate of speed; it was Sunday and there were many people on the road. I begged the boy not to kill anyone.

When we got to the village, we found Dr. Reed's car had been returned, and he had started toward Elkhorn Lodge. So we turned around; with the siren and the gong going full blast, we tore back to the Lodge.

I've never been able to find out whether that boy was a member of Al Capone's gang or just a private citizen. How did he happen to have all of that paraphernalia on his car?

To everyone's surprise and pleasure, the injured boy was conscious, and the next day appeared no worse for his experience, except that he was minus a good deal of skin and had many bruises.

Young guests at a costume party.

Dr. Reed's wife was the former Eleanor Bissell, who with her parents, had been a guest several summers at the Lodge. She is now Eleanor Reed of Golden Horse Ranch.

The best show we put on was one with a stage coach. All the women and children who rode in the coach were dressed as guests of the gay 1880s. Harry Lovern was on the box, and beside sat Mr. Peebles of Cincinnati.

About ten boys were dressed as Indians. They wore khaki trousers with a fringe of khaki sewed down the side seams by Ella Kramer, my wonderful housekeeper. The boys were bare from their waists up, generously smeared with dark stain I had gotten at Riverside. Around their heads they wore bands with turkey feathers stuck in them. The same number of riders were dressed as cowboys.

The stagecoach took a tour of the village, not forgetting to drive by the Stanley Hotel. Then as the coach returned and came within the grounds of the Elkhorn, the Indians, who had been concealed

ENTERTAINMENT AT ELKHORN

Elkhorn guests crowd around the stagecoach in front of the Lodge.
IMAGE COURTESY OF ESTES PARK MUSEUM. 2009.32.009

in the tenthouse colony, swooped down across the lawn, yelling like Comanches. They surrounded the stage, pulled the people out, and, as I afterward discovered, were a little rough with Mr. Peebles.

Just as they were about to start scalping, the cowboys, who had hidden behind the old Lodge, came to the rescue. It certainly was a wild scene; everybody was yelling; riders were falling off their horses.

Eventually, the passengers got back in the stage coach, and it headed back toward town with the Indians behind and the cowboys bringing up the rear.

The whole performance hadn't taken over an hour. After going through town, the stagecoach and riders drove in front of the Stanley Hotel as much as to say, "You are the big hotel, but at the Elkhorn, we have fun!"

It was amazing that nobody got hurt; although it had never been rehearsed, it was considered a great success. But we never did it again.

Entrance to Elkhorn Lodge. The original lodge building is on the right. Straight ahead is the "new" two-storey lodge, build in 1900 with further additions completed in 1907 and 1912.
IMAGE COURTESY OF ESTES PARK MUSEUM. 2009.032.005

Once a year, we had a cabaret; this was held in the dining room of the Lodge. All the big tables were pushed back, and around the edge of the room tables for two and four people were set up. Again the young girls and children, dressed as waitresses, served punch and wafers. The punch consisted of lemon juice, sugar, ginger ale, and plenty of tea. The middle of the floor was sprinkled with cornmeal for dancing.

I can only remember a few of the solos put on; one was by Gussie Busch of St. Louis, who did a dance as a caveman, clothed only in a coyote skin he had taken from the wall of the Lodge. He certainly did a wild dance!

William Michaels of Tulsa, Oklahoma, who had a wonderful voice, did a perfect imitation of Maurice Chevalier. Then there were eight of the guests who danced the minuet. There were other

ENTERTAINMENT AT ELKHORN

numbers, too, but I can't remember them. Between numbers, the audience danced.

We always ended the evening with the "Bachelor's Dream." We chose one of the goodlooking young bachelors, who sat in an easy chair, dressed in his smoking jacket. The occasion was the night before his marriage, and he dreamed of all the sweethearts in his life.

At the other side of the stage area, a man with a good voice would read a verse announcing the numbers in the tableau. I know that two years Mr. Paul Bakewell of St. Louis read these verses for us.

Between the two men was a large frame covered with black cloth, and fitted with black curtains, which could be pulled before each picture. An electrician put a big spotlight in each corner of the frame, so that when the curtain was pulled, one got a splendid view of the occupant.

First came a little girl, about five or six years old, dressed in her daintiest dress. Next, there was the schoolgirl, with her school books, nibbling an apple. Then the girl with whom the young man had gone skating or skiing. During vacation, he was supposed to travel, and would go West, always to Elkhorn Lodge. There he would meet the cowgirl and the Indian maiden.

His next journey would be to a foreign country; if he went to the Orient, there would be the girl he met in Hawaii, the maiden of Japan, and the Chinese girl.

On his return to college, there would be the college widow, dressed in a ravishing black dress. Then he would go to the Continent, where he met the English girl, the French girl, the Dutch girl, the maiden of Switzerland, and the Italian girl. Between each of these pictures, Mr. Bakewell would read a verse to introduce the girls.

At last the bachelor disposes of his pipe, stands up, goes toward the picture frame. When the curtain is drawn, there stands his bride-to-be in all her bridal finery. He takes her by the hand, and she steps out of the frame to meet him.

81

Of course, this tableau required a great deal of work in securing the girls and the costumes they had to wear.

But it was very lovely, and always ended the cabaret.

One year I hired a bulldozer to scoop out a swimming pool where the present paddock at Elkhorn Lodge is located. Men worked for several days building up and packing the banks, and making a sandy beach at one end. They created the first hotel swimming [pool] in Estes Park.

The water which fed the pool trickled down through the corral and the garden; the overflow drained from the pool into the river nearby. I thought the summer sun would warm the water en route to the pool.

As soon as the pool was completed, I included a description of the new swimming facilities in advertising for the Elkhorn. In June, while the air was still quite cool, a young lady and her mother arrived at the Lodge. Almost immediately, the young woman asked me to show her the new swimming pool, which I did.

The next morning I followed her out to the pool as she went for an early morning swim. She stood on the bank near the deep end of the pool for a few moments, then executed a beautiful dive into the water.

There followed a threshing and churning of the water as the young woman paddled frantically to the edge of the pool. She pulled herself out of the water, and stood shivering violently.

"Was it cold?" I asked.

"Like icewater," she exclaimed through chattering teeth. It was her first and last swim in the pool at Elkhorn.

For a few years after that, the pool remained, although only the hardy ventured into it. Mrs. Ashbaugh, now of Littleton, and her friends, were among those who continued to enjoy the pool the years it was in existence.

ENTERTAINMENT AT ELKHORN

Although not many of them used it, the guests at Elkhorn Lodge were the first to be offered swimming facilities in the Estes Park area.

∽

Every once in a while the guests would beg me to make some taffy, and I remember one taffy pull when I buttered the plates for sixty-five guests, and filled them with taffy. When it had cooled enough to be pulled, they were all called in.

Never have I seen a worse conglomeration of taffy. Some of it was white as they pulled it, some of it was sticky. But most of it disappeared, for every little while each taffy puller would take a bite. Whatever was left was cut into little pieces and distributed among the guests.

I did not do this very often. It made the chef cross, because of the sticky pots that had to be washed, and it made the waitresses cross because there was taffy distributed all around the dining room.

∽

Almost every fall after a busy summer, with the closing of the Lodge scheduled in a few days, we would give a Harvest Moon party.

We went into the woods and brought large branches of colored aspen and decorated the living room with them. That evening, the guests were told to disappear and not come back until eleven or later.

Two long tables were brought from the dining room and placed at either end of the living room. One table held chafing dishes of lobster Newberg and creamed mushrooms; platters of fried chicken, sliced ham, roast beef, and tongue; all sorts of salads, olives, preserves, and pickles.

The other table had on it a little keg of cider sitting in a pan of ice, doughnuts, pumpkin pie with whipped cream, mince pie,

The Elkhorn Lodge chef, in apron and cap, about 1900.
IMAGE COURTESY OF ESTES PARK MUSEUM. 2006.040.120.

cream puffs, and several different kinds of cake. The chef was always in charge, dressed in his white uniform and his tall white cap.

Then the guests, who had been dancing in the village or playing cards in their rooms, would appear. They soon made short work of the bounty on the tables.

The Harvest Moon party ended the season at Elkhorn.

CHAPTER SEVEN

Elkhorn Guests

We had at Elkhorn an old register that went back to 1880, and each summer we had to bring it out so that returning guests could pore over it to find out when they were at the Elkhorn twenty, thirty, or even forty years before. Sometimes a couple who had come to the Lodge on their honeymoon would be pathetically disappointed because we were not able to assign them the same room they had had years before.

Of course, I think all of my guests were nice people. Some gave me more trouble than others, but when I would run into them in Denver or some other city, they always looked good to me because they had been my guests.

I wish I could remember all of them by name; however, I would like to mention a few who were prominent.

Mr. Floyd Mechem and his family. Mr. Mechem was Dean of the Law School at Ann Arbor, and at the University of Chicago.

Dr. Thomas D. Wood and his wife. Dr. Wood was in charge of the Horace Mann school at Columbia University, and was the first appointee to the Child Welfare Committee named by President Hoover.

We also had as our guests Mrs. Otis Skinner and her daughter, Cornelia Otis Skinner. Also Maude Adams [sic] of Hull House in Chicago.

Also: Mr. Emerson of Brush, Mr. and Mrs. Prussing of Chicago, Mrs. Vernon Smith of Kansas, Katharine Clark Wolcott of Chicago, Julia Mattis Cone of Moline, Ill. and Sue Conkling of Cincinnatti. Others I remember well were: Nina Cullinen [sic] of Dallas [sic], Texas; and Marian Lewis of New Canaan, Conn.; also the Robert C. Corleys and the Charles Lamys of Clayton, Mo.

There was Senator McKinley of Illinois, and Mr. Will Hays, who was President Taft's campaign manager, then Postmaster General, and still later the "Czar of the movies."

There was a Mr. J. E. Cox and his family of Evansville, Ind.; Mr. McClelland, president of the U. S. Biscuit Co.; and Mr. Craft and his family. Mr. Craft was president of the Harris Bank and Trust Co. of Chicago.

Mrs. Clark Blickensderfer and family did not stay at the Elkhorn, but came to the Lodge often for luncheon or dinner. I feel they should be included with my guests.

Count deRosa was one of our most interesting guests; he came to the Lodge for several summers. He spent almost every day riding horseback, and was an excellent horseman. He was a tall dark man; the horse he chose from the stable was equally dark.

While he was having his breakfast in the morning, he read his newspaper. Then the baker would send to his table a loaf of French bread about eight inches long. When the Count had finished his breakfast, he would cut the loaf, and scrape out the center. Crumbs flew in all directions.

ELKHORN GUESTS

When the loaf was hollowed out, the Count would butter the inside of it, then put a three-egg omelet into the buttered shell. He wrapped the loaf in a piece of his newspaper, and placed the package in his jacket pocket. Then he would go to the barn, get his horse, and ride off for the day. The omelet-filled loaf of French bread was his noon meal.

Count deRosa had been in the consular service with the Italian government for many years. When any one asked his nationality, he would say, "I am a Roman citizen; I was born in Rome on the banks of the Tiber. The doctors were having a difficult time getting me into this world. I heard them say, 'Either this child or his mother must be sacrificed.' When I heard this, I put forth my best efforts, and I was born."

Then there was Dr. William Nitze and his family. He was Dean of Romance Languages at Chicago University. His daughter is Mrs. Walter Paepcke, who with her husband revived the old Colorado mining town of Aspen as a winter sports and cultural center. His son was Paul H. Nitze, who came to the Lodge with his parents as a boy of about eleven, and returned many times after he was married. Paul Nitze is now our Secretary of the Navy.

Eleanor Hondius, photographed in 1963, shortly after the publication of her Memoirs. IMAGE COURTESY OF ESTES PARK MUSEUM. 1968.005.001

CHAPTER EIGHT

Epilogue

I eventually sold my interest in the Elkhorn Lodge and disposed of the Hondius pipeline.

For several years after leaving the Lodge, I was very lonely. I missed my guests and all the excitement.

In these memoirs I have mentioned only a few of the guests who came to the Elkhorn. Almost every summer, some of them come to the cottage across the stream from the Elkhorn to call on me, and we talk over the good times of former years. In 1965, Elkhorn will have been in existence for ninety years.

As I have said before, I was very fond of my guests. I like to think that they were fond of me, too.

ANNOTATED INDEX

"500," a popular card game derived from Euchre, it was invented around the turn of the 20th century and copyrighted in 1904. Auction bridge largely surpassed 500 in popularity in the 1920s, although it is still widely enjoyed in Canada, New Zealand, and Australia: 39–40

Adams, George (c. 1866–), Elkhorn Lodge employee and brother of Johnny Adams: 31

Adams, John. Likely this refers to John O. Adams (1882–1967), an Estes Park carpenter: 25

Adams, Johnny (1867–1953), local resident and employee at Elkhorn Lodge beginning in 1899. His cabin and adjacent pond were on Fall River Road, west of the Lodge: xiv, 28–29, 31, 54–57

Adams, Maud. *See* Addams, Jane

Addams, Jane (1860–1935), pacifist, suffragist, and winner of the 1931 Nobel Peace Prize, Addams was also co-founder, with Ellen G. Starr, of Hull (Settlement) House in Chicago: 86

Andrews, Edwin B. (1871–1942), husband of Sarah

ANNOTATED INDEX

Morrison and brother-in-law of Abner Sprague. Andrews Creek, Glacier, Pass, and Tarn (and possibly Andrews Peak) in RMNP were named in his honor: 37

Ashbaugh, Carrie Frances McLeod (1875–1935), wife of attorney and county judge Florence "Flor" Ashbaugh (1870–1937): 82

Auxiliary to the Estes Park Protection and Improvement Association (EPPIA): 57–59

Bachelor's Dream, a pantomime performed by guests at Elkhorn Lodge as part of the summer's entertainment in 1914, and for years afterward: 81–82

Baker, Frank E. (1843–) Greeley photographer and real estate agent: xvii

Baldwin, Rev. Edward L. (1861–1925), a clergyman and Moraine Park rancher who often led church services at the Community Building. He and his wife, Flora (1863–1919), had two children: Leroy and Esther: 34

Basket social: 29

Beatrice Creamery, a cold storage warehouse in Littleton that opened in 1903. Since 1985 it has been listed on the National Register of Historic Buildings: 46

Beef tea, recipe: 38

Bessie, Eleanor Estes James's pony: 17

Bierstadt, Albert (1830–1902), German-American landscape painter and member of the Hudson River School. Bierstadt visited Estes Park in the 1870s at the invitation of the Earl of Dunraven and completed several major works, including one of Longs Peak (1889) now owned by the Denver Public Library: 4

Bird, Isabella Lucy (1831–1904), English world traveler and author of *A Lady's Life in the Rockies* (1879). Her written descriptions of the Estes Valley she visited in 1873 brought the beauties of the Rocky Mountains to the attention of the world: 6

Bissell, Eleanor Anderson. *See* **Reid, Eleanor Anderson Bissell**

Bissell, Mr. (b. 1858) and Mrs. Morris, a Denver couple and parents of Eleanor Bissell Reid. Mr. Morris was president (1912) of the Denver-based Vulcan Iron Wagon Co.: 77–78

Blickensderfer, Elizabeth (1888–1983), wife of photographer Clark Blickensderfer (1882–1962), who rose to prominence at home and abroad through his mountain landscape and ornithological images, many of which were taken in Rocky Mountain National Park. Both were long-time summer residents of Estes Park: 86

Bond, Cornelius H. (1854–1931), president of the Estes Park Town Company, who arranged for the purchase of property from John Cleave to establish a village at the confluence of the Fall and Big Thompson rivers. He also directed the platting of the village

of Estes Park in 1905 and the sale
of lots along Main Street (later
Elkhorn Avenue). His many contributions are remembered today
in the downtown park that bears
his name: 57

**Boos, Dr. Margaret "Peggy" B.
Fuller (1892–1978).** A geologist,
engineer, scientist, and long-time
Estes Park summer resident who
created natural history programs
as Rocky Mountain National
Park's chief naturalist (1926–1927).
Among her many contributions
to her field was the establishment
of the Department of Geology
at the University of Denver in
1935. "Peggy's Peak," a mountain
in the Talkeetna Mountains of
central Alaska, was named in her
honor: 67

Booze, Dr. Fuller. *See* **Boos, Dr.
Margaret "Peggy" B. Fuller**

Borden, Ellen Walter (1907–1972),
daughter of John Borden. Ellen
married Adlai E. Stevenson II in
1928. The couple later divorced:
19. *See also* **Stevenson, Adlai
Ewing**

Borden, John (1884–1961), eldest
child of William and Mary
DeGarmo Whiting Borden: 19

Borden, Mary (1886–1968): 19. *See
also* **Spears, Lady Mary Borden**

**Borden, Mary DeGarmo Whiting
(1861–1934),** wife of William
Borden: 19

Borden, William (1850–1906),
made his fortune from silver
mines in Colorado. He and Mary
were the parents of four children:

John, Mary, William Whiting,
and Alice Joyce: 19

**Borden, William Whiting
(1887–1913),** a prominent member of the 19th-century Student
Volunteer Movement for Foreign
Missions. Born into the wealthy
Borden family of Chicago, he was
educated at the Hill (PA) School,
Yale University, and Princeton
Theological Seminary. Drawn to
a religious calling by his mother's
evangelism, Borden became a
missionary, dying in Egypt at the
age of 25: 19

*Borden of Harvard. See Borden of
Yale*

Borden of Yale, a biography of
William Whiting Borden by
Geraldine G. Taylor. It was first
published by the Moody Press in
1913 and is still in print: 19

Boyd, Alexander (1876–1975), a
Chicago banker who, with his wife
Louise, was a guest at Elkhorn
Lodge in 1911. The couple eventu-
ally retired to Estes Park: 40

Busch, Gussie. *See* **Busch, August
"Gussie" Anheuser, Jr.**

**Busch, August "Gussie" Anheuser,
Jr. (1899–1989).** Heir to a St.
Louis brewing fortune founded
in 1869 by his grandfather, Gussie
worked his way up from laborer
to Chairman of the Board, a position he held from 1946–1975: 80

**Campfire Girls Camp in Estes
Park.** The Earl of Dunraven's
summer home on Fish Creek was
eventually transformed into a

ANNOTATED INDEX

summer camp for Campfire Girls, a national organization founded in Washington D.C. in 1912: 4

Carmack, Wilfred Earl (1891–1980), was for a time in charge of the Park Service's own telephone system in Rocky Mountain National Park: 53

Carroll, Lewis, pen name of Charles L. Dodgson (1832–1898), English author and mathematician: 15

Casey. A reference to the song *And the Band Played On*, written in 1895 by John H. Palmer: 29

Casino at Elkhorn Lodge: xiv, 21

Chapin, Frederick Hastings (1852–1900), Connecticut-born mountaineer, amateur archaeologist, author, and photographer, for whom Mt. Chapin was named: xvi, 10–11. *See also* **Chapin, Mt.**

Chapin, Mt. (alt. 12,454'), one of three peaks (with Mt. Chiquita and Mt. Ypsilon) of the southern part of the Mummy Range, now within Rocky Mountain National Park. It was named for Frederick Hasting Chapin. In his book *Mountaineering in Colorado,* Chapin credits his wife Alice with the naming of Mt. Ypsilon: xiv, 10

Chapman, Areanna "Arah" (Mrs. Alson C.)(1851–1936), sister of Abner Sprague, rented cabins in Moraine Park, and owned a small store, which also served as the community's post office: 29

Chevalier, Maurice Auguste (1888–1972), internationally-known French actor and entertainer: 80

Chez Jay Building, Estes Park. The Chez Jay Café and Lounge was opened in 1938. With its art deco design and Himalayan motifs, the restaurant was a novelty in Estes Park: 32

Cleave, John (1839–1925). An English-born carpenter, Cleave helped Theodore Whyte build the Earl of Dunraven's Estes Park Hotel. John and his wife Margaret E. May (1845–1921) and two children, Paul and Virginia, lived in one of the first permanent buildings in Estes Park. Cleave survived into the 20th century, selling his property to Bond and associates for the building of the town in 1905. John and Margaret are buried in the Cleave-Griffith Family Cemetery, located at 1700 Colorado Highway 66, on land once owned by Albin Griffith: 23-24, 27, 30–33

Cleave, Virginia (1885–1936), married (1906) John Griffith, the son of Albin and Margaret Griffith: 30

Cleve. *See* **Cleave, John T.**

Cole, Harry G. (b.1863), a rancher, who, for a time, owned a resort (Cole's Place) on Cabin Creek near Allenspark: 19–20

Cone, Julia Rebecca Mattis (1879–1969) of Moline, Illinois, wife of Ross R. Mattis, and niece of Republican Representative and U.S. Senator from Illinois William Brown McKinley (1856–1926). The Mattis family summered at Elkhorn Lodge in 1909, 1910, and 1912: 86

ANNOTATED INDEX

Conesius, St. *See* **Conisius, St. Peter**

Conisius, St. Peter (1521–1597), the patron saint of Germany, was a prolific writer and an important figure in the Catholic Reformation throughout Europe. Born in Nijmegen, he was first Dutchman to join the Society of Jesus. Conisius was responsible for adding the line, "Holy Mary, Mother of God, Pray for us sinners, now and at the hour of our death," to the Rosary and was canonized in 1925: 48

Conkling, Susan B (1886–1984), a Cincinnati socialite: 86

Corley, Mr. and Mrs. Robert C., were from Clayton Missouri: 86

Cox, James Emery (1883–1963) and his wife Helen, visited the Elkhorn Lodge from their home in Evansville, Indiana: 70, 86

Craft, Mr.: 86

Crocker, Frank Walter (1846–1932), purchased land and buildings at the base of Mt. Olympus, establishing a ranch there. The Crockers were regular visitors at the Elkhorn Lodge throughout the 1880s and 1890s and prominent members of the Estes community: xvi, 6

Crocker, Helen Malone (1851–1933), wife of Frank Walter Crocker: xiv, 11

Crocker, Sherwood (1876–1962), son of F. W. Crocker: xvi, 11, 31

Crocker Ranch, located beneath Mt. Olympus in Estes Park, off today's Highway 36: 38

Cullinan, Nina (1896–1983), was a patroness of public parks and the arts in Houston, Texas, and a benefactor of the Houston Ballet and the Houston Symphony Orchestra. Born in Pennsylvania the heiress to an oil fortune, Nina grew up in Houston. Cullinan Hall of the Houston Museum of Fine Arts, a building designed by Ludwig Mies van der Rohe, was named in honor of her financial support. Nina first visited Elkhorn Lodge with her family in 1919, later purchasing land off today's Rock Ridge Road, immediately east of the Lodge: 86

Cunnings, Sir. *See* **Gordon-Cumming, Sir Wiliam Alexander Gordon)**

Dances, dinner: 72–73

Darby, Lorena E. (1914–1993): ix, xix

Davis, Courtney: 72

DeRosa, Count. It is likely that Eleanor refers here to Rolando Dalla Rosa Prati Marquese di Collecchio, an Italian diplomat, appointed Vice Consul in 1932, for counties in southern California, 86–87

District School. *See* **School, Estes Park; School at Elkhorn Lodge.**

Doak, Charles Francis (1897–1967), seasonal chef for the Elkhorn Lodge. His wife, **Margaret Madsen Doak (1884–1955),** was a waitress: 46

Dunraven, Windham Thomas Wyndham-Quin 4th Earl of

ANNOTATED INDEX

(1841–1926), Irish nobleman, who first visited Estes Park in December 1872, and later acquired much of the Estes Valley, where he ranged cattle and built Estes Park's first grand hotel: xiv, 3–6, 8, 10, 30, 32

Dunraven Cottage, the Earl's summer home, located on what is now Fish Creek Road, and built by John Cleave, about 1876: 4

Dunraven Hotel, built in 1877 for the Earl of Dunraven by John Cleave. The hotel, known locally as the "English Hotel" or "The Estes Park Hotel," burned to the ground in August 1911: 4, 5, 30

Elections in Estes Park: 24

Emerson, Mr.: 86

Estes, Joel (1806–1875), Estes Park pioneer. Joel and his son Milton "discovered" the Estes Valley in October 1859; he moved his wife, Patsey Stollings Estes, and their children to the Estes Valley in 1864. Finding the climate unsuitable for cattle raising, the Estes family moved away in 1866. The original Estes cabins were purchased by Griff Evans: 7

Estes Park Bank, the first brick structure in the village opened in 1908: 23

Estes Park Country Club: 37, 73

Estes Park Library. The library was founded by the Estes Park Woman's Club in 1914: xviii, 59, 60

Estes Park, Literary Society of. A turn-of-the-century social group

made up of Estes Park residents and their guests, it was organized about 1900 by Johnny Adams and Louise Tallant and numbered among its members Enos and Joe Mills and Warren Rutledge. Programs included musical evenings, lectures, and literary recitations: 28–29

Estes Park Protective and Improvement Association (EPPIA), a businessmen's organization that made regulations, established public policy, and identified projects for civic improvements, including a local fish hatchery, before the incorporation of the Town of Estes Park in 1917: 57, 58

Estes Park Woman's Club, founded in 1912, raised money for all kinds of civic and preservation projects. Among its charter members were the most prominent women in Estes Park: 59, 60, 67

Evans, Griffith J. "Griff" (1832–1900), a Welshman who moved to the Estes Valley in 1867 and took over the cabins built by Joel Estes near Fish Creek. The property was later sold to the Earl of Dunraven: 5–6, 9, 30

Fish Hatchery. Built on Fall River in 1907, the fish hatchery was an early project of the EPPIA: 57–58

Fitzpatrick, Bernard Edward Barnaby, 2nd Baron Castleton (1849–1937), Irish MP and military officer who served in the Boer War: 3

ANNOTATED INDEX

Flagg Family, summer visitors to Elkhorn Lodge from New York: 63–65

Florence, Lady. Lady Florence Farr (1860–1937) was a prominent English actress: 5

Flower Show at the Elkhorn Lodge: 70–71

Fountain Valley School, Colorado Springs. Founded in 1930 as a private boarding school for boys, which featured a progressive curriculum. The school now educates both boys and girls: 50

Frontier Days, Cheyenne, WY: 73

Frumess, Harry A., son of Ben and Clara Frumess, who purchased the studio of nationally-known Estes Park photographer Fred Clatworthy in 1948. Built in 1888 as Estes Park's first school, the building, located in the heart of downtown on Elkhorn Avenue, was re-opened by Ben and Clara as the Pioneer Gift Shop. Harry and his wife Doris ran the shop until 1994: 23

Fuller, Dr. Margaret "Peggy." *See* **Boos, Dr. Margaret "Peggy" B. Fuller**

Garardi, Mr. Most likely, this is a reference to Antonio Gerardi (1891–1973), a prominent music teacher and violinist, who played with the Boston Symphony Orchestra in the 1910s and 1920s: 67

Garner, Mr. John Lake (1864–1941). With his family, Garner was an early guest at the Elkhorn and later purchased the adjacent

William Riddick Whitehead cottage, completed in 1881, just up the hill from the Casino: 27

Geon, David. *See* **Guion, David W.**

Golden Horse Ranch: 77, 78

Gookin, Miss, 55

Gordon-Cumming, Sir William Alexander Gordon (1848–1930), Scottish military officer, adventurer, and socialite. Best remembered as an arrogant womanizer, he was convicted of cheating at baccarat during a game with the Prince of Wales in 1891: 3

Guion, David W. (1892–1981), a music teacher, Broadway actor, and composer: 67–68

Gwin, Ralph. *See* **Gwynn, Walter Ralph**

Gwynn, Walter Ralph (1897–1963). Owner of the Park Theatre built between 1913–1915 in downtown Estes Park, Gwynn added the lobby and the building's iconic 80-foot tower in 1926. The Theatre was added to the National Register of Historic Places in 1984: 61

Gymkhana, an equestrian event, traditionally consisting of races and games: 68, 75–76

"Hare and Hounds": 73

Harvest Moon Party: 83–84

Havemeyer, Theodora (1878–1945). Born in New York, the daughter of a prominent and wealthy family, Theodora married Cameron McRae Winslow in 1899 in Newport, R.I.: 65–66

Hawaii, visits by the Hondius family: 45, 49–50

97

ANNOTATED INDEX

Hayden, Mrs. (1856–1935). Emma Cornelia Howe of Chicago married Albert Hayden (1847–1911) in 1877. The couple had two sons, Albert Jr. (1882–1932) and Julian ("Jude") (1886–1964), who were educated as engineers. Avid outdoorsmen, the sons moved to Estes Park sometime before 1910. Their mother moved west to join her sons after her husband's death in 1911: 55

Hays, William Harrison (1879–1954), politician and movie mogul. Founder (in 1907) of the Harrison Trust and Savings bank, Hays also served as chairman of the Republican National Committee (1918–1921) and as U.S. Postmaster General (1921–1922). Later, he was named president of the Motion Picture Producers and Distributors of America: 86

Heeney, Mrs. Georgiana Needham (1827–1891), was the widow of Thomas Heeney (1821–1865) and mother of Mary Clara, wife of Alexander Quiner MacGregor: 9–10

Hewes, Charles Edwin (1870–1947), an Iowa-born novelist and poet, Hewes homesteaded in the Tahosa Valley with his brother Steve and his mother in 1907. Charlie worked briefly for Enos Mills at nearby Longs Peak Inn; in 1914, the family founded the Hewes-Kirkwood Inn: xviii–xix

Hollebird. It is likely that this is a reference to William Holabird

(1854) and his son, John Augur Holabird (1886–1945). Father and son were Chicago architects: 60

Hondius, Jodocus (1563–1612), Dutch cartographer and engraver: 47

Hondius, Jon Jacobus Puppius Hondius. See **Hondius, Jodocus**

Hondius, Pieter (1864–1934), husband of Eleanor Estes James Hondius of Elkhorn Lodge: xi, xv, xvii, xviii, xxi, 44–45, 47–50, 53, 55

Hondius, Pieter "Pete" Jr. (b. 1923), son of Pieter and Eleanor Estes James Hondius: v, viii, x, xvii, xix–xx, 44, 45, 47, 49–53, 57, 60, 74

Hondius pipeline (1907–1996): 53–54

Hoover, Mrs. Lou Henry Hoover (1874–1944), wife of Herbert Clark Hoover, 31st President of the United States (1929–1933): 59, 86

Huntington Library: 47

Hupp Hotel, a 23-room, 2-storey wooden structure completed in 1907 by Josephine "Josie" Hupp (1857–1931) on the southeast corner of Moraine and Elkhorn avenues. Its downtown location, its basement, and its hot and cold running water made the hotel unique: 59

Husted, Clara Gertrude Crawford (Mrs. Shepherd) (1871–1963): 30

Husted, Shepherd Newcombe "Shep" (1867–1942), was a mountain guide, forest ranger, and innkeeper, who built the Rustic Hotel, located off Devil's Gulch Road, in 1900: 49

ANNOTATED INDEX

Hyde, Miss. It is likely that Eleanor was referring to Mary Roosevelt Hyde, a teacher, and elder sister of Albert Alexander Hyde (1848–1935). A. A. Hyde was a Kansas philanthropist and founder of the Mentholatum Co., and was a major benefactor of the YMCA of the Rockies: 11

Hyde boys. Presumably, Eleanor was referring to the two youngest sons of A. A. and Ida E. Todd Hyde, Paul H. Hyde and George A. Hyde: 72

In the Shade of the Old Apple Tree **(1905)**, popular song, words by Harry Williams and music by Egbert Van Alstyne: 29

James, Charles W. "Charlie" (1869–1889), brother to Howard, Homer, and Eleanor James: 7–9, 14

James, Ella McCabe (1843–1917), wife of William E. James and mother to Eleanor and her three brothers; two additional children died in infancy: xvi, 7–10

James, Homer Edward (1866–1958). Educated as a physician, he gave up practicing at an early date in order to purchase several local businesses, including a lumberyard. In 1905 married Jennie Chapin, who for a number of years ran a mercantile at the corner of Elkhorn and Moraine avenues with Elizabeth (E.M.A.) Foot: xv, 7, 8, 9, 34–39

James, Howard Perry (1874–1928), operated Elkhorn Lodge with his mother and sister following the death of his father: xv, 7, 8, 9, 31, 36, 37, 39–45, 47, 66

James, William Edwin (1842–1895), father of Eleanor Estes James Hondius and founder of the Elkhorn Lodge. His hunting prowess provided the Lodge with its signature pile of elk horns: xiii, xvi, 7–11, 36

Jefferson, Joe. An American actor (1825–1905) and avid fisherman, Jefferson summered regularly in Estes Park at the turn of the 20th century: 4, 5

Johnson Boys, the single brothers Edward (b. 1874) and Charles (b. 1880) Johnson, sons of local farmer and rancher Julius A. Johnson, and his wife, Ella (b. 1867). The brothers leased the MacGregor Ranch after Donald MacGregor's death, from 1901–1907: 32–33

Jones, Freda (1890–1975), wife of Elmer Jones, a local carpenter: 55

Jones, Rita. *See* **Jones, Freda**

Jones, Stannie Rebecca (b. 1892), wife of Walter R. Jones and sister-in-law of Freda Jones: 55

K&B Packing & Provision Co. was located in Denver: 52

Kramer, Ellen Elizabeth "Ella" (1888–1971): 46

Lamb, Carlyle (1862–1958), noted local mountain climber and guide and son of Elkanah Lamb

ANNOTATED INDEX

and his first wife, Welta Jane "Hattie" Lamb (d. 1867): 38

Lamb, Emma Eleanor Batchelder (Mrs. Carlyle) (1855–1936): 38

Lamb, Jemima Jane Spencer Lamb (Mrs. Elkanah J.) (1829–1917): 25, 26, 28

Lamb, Rev. Elkanah (1832–1915), minister affiliated with the Church of the United Brethren who held services at the Community Church in Estes Park for many years. Author of *Memories of the Past and Thoughts of the Future,* Lamb was also an accomplished mountain climber and professional guide. His Longs Peak House was sold in 1901, by his son Carlyle, to Enos A. Mills, who erected his own resort on the site a year later: xiv, 25–28

Lamy, Charles S. (1905–1987) and his wife Julia Walsh (1914–1987), were from St. Louis, where Mr. Lamy was a prominent banker and civic leader. The couple purchased a home in Estes Park, located above the Elkhorn Lodge property on Rock Ridge Rd. Their daughters Judy (1907–2007) and Mary (1938–) were longtime residents of Estes Park; it was Judy Lamy who donated the land for Mrs. Walsh's Garden, which lies below her property and now belongs to the Town. The Garden was named in honor of Judy's grandmother, Winifred Walsh: 86

Longs Peak Inn, a Tahosa Valley resort built in 1902 by the naturalist Enos Abijah Mills. The site first belonged to Elkanah Lamb and later his son Carlyle; Mills took over the Lamb's Longs Peak house and renamed it. The main lodge building at the Inn, but not the outbuildings, burned to the ground in 1906. Mills rebuilt it immediately. In its heyday, the Inn enjoyed a national reputation. Situated as it was at the foot of Longs Peak, it was a favorite of mountain climbers as well as those wishing to escape from city life. When Mills died in 1922, his wife Esther Burnell ran the Inn until it was destroyed by fire in 1947: 19, 38

Lovern, Harry C. (1887–1967): 76–78

Macdonald, Jessica Chapin (1874–1957) (Mrs. Julius Edward), who established a small business on Elkhorn Avenue, where she sold gifts, office supplies, and books. She was a founding member (1912) of the Woman's Club. Her store became Macdonald's Book Shop, which continues under the ownership of Jessica's granddaughter, Paula Steige: 56

MacGregor, Alexander Quiner (1846–1896), a newspaperman from Wisconsin, who homesteaded in the Black Canyon and founded the ranch that bears his name: xiii, 9–10

MacGregor, Maria Clara Heeney (1852–1901), an accomplished artist, who married A. Q. MacGregor in 1873, and who, with the help of her three sons (George, Donald,

100

ANNOTATED INDEX

and Halbert), operated the ranch after her husband's death. She served briefly (1876–77) as Estes Park postmistress and operated the ranch store: 9

McClelland, Mr. U.S. Biscuit Company: 86

McCreery, Rev. William H. (1839–1926), a Presbyterian missionary who homesteaded in the Estes Valley in 1874. McCreery originally settled on property on the Fall River, which he subsequently swapped with William E. James for land beneath Lumpy Ridge off today's Devils Gulch Road: xiii, 50–51

McCreery Ranch: 8

McGrew, Emily Claire Foot (1880–1948), London-born wife of Samuel Finley McGrew, ran a gift shop on Elkhorn Avenue, c. 1900. She was the sister of Elizabeth Mary Ann Foot (b. 1876), who also had a shop in early Estes Park, and sister-in-law to Rose Elizabeth McGrew, an internationally known opera singer: 68–69

McGrew, George T. (1907–1992), son of Samuel and Emily Clair McGrew: 55

McGrew, Rosa Elizabeth (1874–1956), born in Iowa to Elizabeth P. and William A. McGrew, Rose grew up in Denver where she studied voice. Encouraged to pursue her studies abroad, Rose traveled to Europe in 1894, later performing in opera and on the concert stage in Berlin and Dresden. Upon returning to

Denver, she taught voice, and eventually moved to Portland, where she joined the voice faculty at the University of Oregon, 1920–1947. In Oregon, she was known as "Madame Rose." Her brother, Samuel Finley McGrew, married Emily Claire Foot of Estes Park: 68–69

McKinley, William Brown (1856–1926), banker, philanthropist, University trustee, and Republican congressman who served Illinois in both the United States House of Representatives (1914–1921) and the Senate (1921–1926): 86

Meadowdale Stock Ranch, part of the Crocker Ranch: 6

Mechem, Floyd Russell (1858–1928), Tappan Professor of Law at the University of Michigan (1982–1903) and later Professor of Law at Chicago University. He authored many books and journal articles on the law and his profession, and with his wife Jessie Collier Russell, had two sons, John and Phillip. The Mechems were regular visitors to the Elkhorn Lodge between 1905 and 1910: 86

Michaels, William Clopton, (1871–1963), a Kansas City, Missouri, attorney. He, his wife Nancy Stone Wilson, and their sons, William and Eldon, were frequent summer guests at the Elkhorn Lodge between 1912 and 1920. The elder William was an active participant and winner at auction bridge, during tournaments

ANNOTATED INDEX

held at the Elkhorn, and his son William was featured as a singer and impressionist in Elkhorn's cabaret evenings: 80

Mills, Enos Abijah (1870–1922), a largely self-taught naturalist, preservationist, professional mountain guide, and successful innkeeper, Mills is chiefly remembered today as a prime mover in the establishment of Rocky Mountain National Park. A nephew of Elkanah Lamb, Mills had come to Estes Park as a boy in 1885, building his own tiny homestead cabin at the base of the Twin Sister Mountain. In 1902 he opened the Longs Peak Inn on the site of Lamb's Longs Peak House, just across the valley from his cabin. In 1918 Mills married Esther Burnell (1889–1964), who had proved up her own homestead claim, before becoming his secretary and a sort of protégé in the business of nature guiding, which Mills himself pioneered. The couple had one child, a daughter Enda, the following year: xiv, 3, 25, 27–28

Muggins Gulch, a ravine south of Estes Park, on the road to Lyons, and site of James Nugent's (Rocky Mountain Jim's) cabin: 6, 25

Mugwumps: persons who left the Republican Party in 1884, or, persons not affiliated or committed to a particular political party: 25

New York Poly-Clinic (Graduate Medical School and Hospital) opened in 1882 to provide postgraduate program for physicians.

Originally located on East 34th Street, the school offered its students hands-on medical experiences, providing free medical care for patients. The faculty was made up of prominent New York doctors. Later the school merged with Columbia University College of Physicians and Surgeons: 35

Nitze, Paul H. (1907–2004), politician and Cold War strategist who served as the Secretary of the Navy from 1963–67. Known as "the Silver Fox," Nitze was a creator of the "policy of containment" as a way to thwart the expansion of communism in the post–World War II era. After his retirement, he was instrumental in developing Aspen as a skiing destination. Nitze's sister Elizabeth, and her husband Walter Paepcke, initially developed plans to make Aspen a sports, arts, and cultural center, recruiting investors for the Aspen Skiing Corp (1945). Nitze's investment of $75,000 made him the largest shareholder: 87

Nitze, William Albert (1876–1957), father of Paul H. Nitze, was a college professor and research scholar specializing in Old French literature and romance languages at Amherst, the University of California, and the University of Chicago. His family summered at the Elkhorn in 1920, where Mrs. Nitze chaperoned dances at the Estes Park Country Club: 87

ANNOTATED INDEX

Nugent, James ("Rocky Mountain Jim") (d. 1874), mountain guide and legendary paramour of the international traveler Isabella Bird during her visit to Estes Park in 1873: 6

Old Man Mountain. *See* **Oldman Mountain**

Oldman Mountain, the peak that rises directly behind Elkhorn Lodge. It was named by members of the Arapohoe tribe during their visit to the Estes Valley in 1914: 18

One-armed bandits: 71–72

Paepcke, Elizabeth Nitze (1902–1994), daughter of Professor William Albert Nitze, Elizabeth attended the Chicago Art Institute and went on to design theatres. The intellectual contacts through her father and the international contacts through her diplomat brother Paul H. Nitze were important in the Paepckes' success in making Aspen a cultural center: 87

Paepcke, Walter Paul (1896–1960) was a wealthy Chicago industrialist, whose philanthropic contributions included the founding of the Aspen Institute and the Aspen Music Festival and School. In 1926, Paepcke founded the Container Corporation of America. He married William Nitze's daughter Elizabeth in 1922, and the couple worked together to develop Aspen's literary and musical programs and festivals: 87

Paepke, Walter. See **Paepcke, Walter Paul**

Patsy, Eleanor Hondius' horse: 19–21

Pauley, Peter "P.J." Jr. (1854–1935), a local, St. Louis–born rancher, who had served briefly as a hunting guide for the Earl of Dunraven and later purchased land along Cow Creek from Hank Farrar. Pauley's ranch, the Double Bar Y, was sold in 1897. The McGraws leased and then purchased the property in 1908. Today, the ranch has been preserved by its owner, the National Park Service, which uses it as a research facility: 70

Pauley Cottage: 63

Peary, Rear Admiral Robert Edwin (1856–1920), civil engineer, Naval officer, and explorer who was long regarded as the first (1909) to reach the geographical North Pole: 59

Peebles, Joseph Straub (1844–1916), a civil war veteran and prominent Cincinnati businessman. He and his family summered at the Elkhorn at the turn of the century: 78–79

Pettifogging: emphasizing petty details or practicing legal trickery: 9

Pew, Arthur E. Sr. (1875–1916) a founder of the Pew Trust, and husband of Helene Daisy Crocker (1879–1944): 6

Pew, Arthur E., Jr. (1899–1965), son of Arthur and Helene Pew. Arthur, Jr., purchased the Crocker Ranch in 1947: 6

ANNOTATED INDEX

Pew, Walter C. (1901–1989), the younger son of Arthur and Helene Pew, headed the Sun Oil Company for over 40 years: 6

Pioneer Award. The Pioneer Award is presented by the Estes Park Friends & Foundation, Inc. to individuals who have, over time, contributed to the preservation and understanding of the history of the Estes Valley: xvii

Polk, Miss: 67

Prussing, Eugene, Mr. and Mrs.: 86

Ramey, Johnny Bill. John William Ramey (1921–2008), was the son of Ollie J. and Emma Bertha Ramey. Often called "Johnny Bill," Ramey was born in Longmont, and spent his life in the Estes Valley. He helped to build Trail Ridge Road, sold real estate for his family's agency, served on the Town Board, was a former Chief of the Estes Park Fire Departmen, as well as a life member of the Estes Park American Legion Post 119. He was also involved in activities in support of the preservation of MacGregor Ranch and the F. O. Stanley Museum: 51

Ranchhouse. Originally a part of the Earl of Dunraven's holdings in Estes Park, the building became Griffith J. Evans's home after the Earl of Dunraven returned to Ireland c. 1885: 5, 9, 30

Reed, Dr. *See* **Reid, Henry Squire**

Reed, Eleanor Bissell. *See* **Reid, Eleanor Anderson Bissell**

Reid, Eleanor Anderson Bissell (1896–1975), wife of Henry Squire Reid, and the mother of one child, Henry Squire Reid, Jr.: 76–78

Reid, Henry Squire (1886–1974), New York–born physician and surgeon who practiced medicine in Denver and Palm Springs while maintaining a summer practice in Estes Park. In 1917, he married Eleanor Bissell: 76–77

Riddle, J. R. (b. 1859). Stereographer and "Photographic View" photographer from Topeka, Kansas, who maintained an office in Loveland, Colorado, in the 1880s: xvii, 16

Rocky Mountain Jim. *See* **Nugent, James**

Rowe, Isaak. *See* **Rowe, Israel**

Rowe, Israel (1844–1884), an early Estes Park resident and an expert hunter-guide, Rowe homesteaded land below Mount Olympus on what is now the Crocker Ranch. He discovered Rowe Glacier, which was named in his honor: 6, 10

Rudi, Dr. *See* **Rüedi, Dr. Carl**

Rüedi, Dr. Carl (1848–1901) was a world-famous tuberculosis specialist who studied the effects of climate on the treatment of the disease. He came to Colorado from Davos for a brief time, practicing in Denver from 1891–1896. During that period he also operated a tent camp for patients in Estes Park, some of whom came from a sanitarium in the Front Range town of Hygiene: 48

ANNOTATED INDEX

Rutledge, Warren, (1871–1946), a popular Estes Park mountain guide, who emigrated from Ireland in 1896: 29

Sanbon, Burton Davis (1859–1914), Estes landowner who, with F. O. Stanley, purchased Dunraven's Estes Park holdings in 1908: 4

School, Estes Park. Presumably the reference is to the town's first public school, a log structure built in 1907 and located behind today's Bond Park. It was replaced in 1919 by a larger school building, erected on the same site: 23–24, 25

School at Elkhorn Lodge. William James hired Dr. Judson Ellis, one of the Elkhorn's employees, to teach his children, using one of the Lodge's cabins for this purpose. The cabin is still in existence: 11, 23

Side-saddle, a saddle style that allows the rider to sit "aside" rather than "astride" her horse: 20, 21

"Silver Threads among the Gold," (1873), song written by H. P. Danks and Eben E. Rexford, popular in the late 19th and early 20th centuries: 29

Size, John Henry (1847–1941). According to an article in *Estes Park Trail*, April 1923, Uncle John was a regular summer visitor beginning in 1886 and "never missed a season": 60–61

Skinner, Cornelia Otis (1899–1979), author, Broadway actress, and humorist, was a guest at the Elkhorn Lodge in July 1907. Her father was Otis Skinner (1858–1942), a noted stage and movie actor: 86

Smith, Mrs. Vernon: 86

Spears, Lady Mary Borden (1886–1968), American expatriate and internationally-known author. She is also remembered for her work as manager of a major French hospital during the WWI battle of the Somme: 19

Sprague, Abner Erwin (1850–1943). With his father Thomas Sprague, Abner homesteaded in Moraine Park in 1876, building the Sprague Hotel, which he sold to J.D. Stead in 1902. In 1914, Abner and Alberta built Sprague's Lodge in Glacier Basin: xiii, 4–6

Sprague, Fred Harmon (1857–1922), brother of Abner Sprague: 34

Sprague, Mary Alberta Morrison (Mrs. Abner) (1867–1949): 29

Stanley, Flora Jane Record (1847–1939), wife of F. O. Stanley. The couple married on April 15, 1876: 55, 59, 60, 67

Stanley, Freelan Oscar "F. O." (1849–1940), Maine-born inventor and entrepreneur, who, with his twin brother F. E. Stanley, invented the Stanley Dry Plate photographic process and the Stanley Steam Car. Stanley arrived to Estes Park in 1903 seeking relief from tuberculosis, and stayed the night at Elkhorn Lodge. After several summers at

ANNOTATED INDEX

the Elkhorn, he and Flora built their own summer home, and a grand hotel, opened in 1909: xvii, 4, 57

Stanley Hotel, a 4-storey Georgian Style frame structure and Estes Park landmark. Built by F. O. Stanley in 1909, it was the first all-electric hotel west of the Mississippi River: 78–79

Stanley Steam Car, invented by F. O. Stanley and his twin brother, Francis Edgar Stanley: 64

Stevenson, Adlai Ewing, II (1900–1965), Harvard-educated lawyer, politician, Governor of Illinois 1949–1953, Presidential candidate in 1952 and 1956, and Ambassador to the United Nations (1961–1965): 19

Stone, Rev. John Timothy Stone, (1868–1954), prominent Chicago Presbyterian clergyman, who built (1920) Mountainside Lodge, a log home at the YMCA or the Rockies: 66

Storer, George (1899–1975), Ohio-born broadcasting pioneer and philanthropist, who maintained a home in Estes Park that became known as the Storer Ranch: 72

Stuyvesant, Elizabeth Ten Eyck, wife of John Reade Stuyvesant: 6

Stuyvesant, John Reade (b. 1850), stayed at the Elkhorn Lodge in 1884, purchased the ranch at the foot of Mount Olympus four years later from pioneer Israel Rowe. In 1899, the property was sold to F. W. Crocker: 6

Stuyvesant, Peter (1610–1672): 6

Surcingle. A wide strap that runs under the belly of a horse to hold a blanket in place: 76

Sweep, Channing. *See* **Sweet, Channing Fullerton**

Sweet, Channing Fullerton (1898–1994), son of William Ellery and Joyeuse Lennig Fullerton Sweet. William Sweet, soon to become Governor of the state of Colorado, was the first member of his family to stay at the Elkhorn Lodge. He later purchased an 160-acre property off Fish Creek, near the site of the Earl of Dunraven's English Hotel: 72

Swift Packing Co.: 46

Taffy-pull: 83

Talent, Lee. *See* **Tallant, Lee**

Tallant, Lee (1888–1959), son of Judge Richard Tallant (1853–1934) a local artist, merchant, and justice of the peace: 29

Tallant, Rhoda Service (1895–1981), wife of Lee Tallant: 29

Toll, Roger Wolcott (1883–1936). Toll and his wife Marguerite were Elkhorn Lodge guests in 1911. He later served as superintendent of Rocky Mountain National Park from 1921–1929: 49

Tolle, Roger. *See* **Toll, Roger Wolcott**

Tommy, the James family's cat: 10, 13, 15

Topliff, Dr. Joseph Jerome (1832–1895). A graduate of Dartmouth Medical College and Bellevue

ANNOTATED INDEX

Hospital Medical College (1886), Topliff practiced in Boulder and Longmont: 35

Toploff, Dr. *See* **Topliff, Dr.**

Town and Country (Magazine). Founded in 1846 as the *Home Journal*, *Town and Country* is the oldest continuously published magazine in the country: 66

Townsend, Florine (1898–1986): 44

Uncle John. *See* **Size, John Henry**

Ute Tribe. Several bands of Utes originally inhabited the mountains of Colorado, until they were relocated elsewhere: 73

Vail, Agnes. *See* **Vaille, Agnes Wolcott**

Vaille, Agnes Wolcott (1890–1925), Smith-educated member of the Colorado Mountain Club, who lost her life attempting a winter climb of Longs Peak. She was a cousin of Roger Toll, the RMNP Superintendent: 49

Visit, Arapahoe (1914). The Indians invited to Estes Park to establish place names were Gus Griswold and Sherman Sage; a third tribe member, Tom Crispen, acted as interpreter: 49

Voting in Estes Park: 24–25

White, William Allen, Jr. *See* White, William Lindsay

White, William Lindsay (1900–1973), son of Pulitzer Prize winning author, journalist, and editor (*The Emporia Gazette*) William Allen White (1868–1944), whose family summered in a stone cabin in Moraine Park between 1905–1944: 72

Wight, Ida E., a guest at the Elkhorn Lodge in September, 1914: 70

Winslow, Rear Admiral Cameron McRae (1854–1932), USN, veteran of the Spanish-American War, World War I, and commander of the Pacific Fleet (1915–1916), summered with his family at Elkhorn Lodge in 1920 and 1921: 65–66

Wolcott, Catherine Garretson (Craft) (1891–1977) Chicago: 85

Wolcott, Katherine Clark. *See* **Wolcott, Catherine Garretson**

Wood, Dr. Thomas Dennison, (1865–1951), founder of the Horace Mann School at Columbia University and a pioneer in physical and health education: 86

Made in the USA
Columbia, SC
05 November 2018